DOOMED GROOMS

GAY AND BISEXUAL HUSBANDS IN STRAIGHT MARRIAGES

BY

BONNIE KAYE, M.Ed.

CCB Publishing
British Columbia, Canada

Doomed Grooms: Gay and Bisexual Husbands in Straight Marriages

Copyright © 2012 by Bonnie Kaye, M.Ed.
ISBN-13: 978-1-77143-021-0
Second Edition

Library and Archives Canada Cataloguing in Publication
Kaye, Bonnie, 1951-
Doomed grooms : gay and bisexual husbands in straight marriages /
by Bonnie Kaye. – 2nd ed.
ISBN 978-1-77143-021-0
Also available in electronic format.
Additional cataloguing data available from Library and Archives Canada

Front Cover an original work of art by Maureen Kavaney Tillman:
http://MaureenTillman.blogspot.com and http://MaureenTillman.etsy.com

Publisher: CCB Publishing
               British Columbia, Canada
               www.ccbpublishing.com

I dedicate this book

- To my Mother, who always gave me faith in myself,

- To my Soulmate of over 18 years who makes me feel beautiful every day,

- To the straight women and gay men who spend years of their lives struggling with the pain of these marriages.

AND…

Special thanks go to my wonderful women who contributed to this book in order to shine lightness in a world that is often dark.

Other books by Bonnie Kaye

The Gay Husband Checklist for Women Who Wonder

Over the Cliff: Gay Husbands in Straight Marriages

ManReaders: A Woman's Guide to Dysfunctional Men

Straight Wives: Shattered Lives (Volume 1)

Straight Wives: Shattered Lives (Volume 2)

Bonnie Kaye's Straight Talk

How I Made My Husband Gay: Myths About Straight Wives

and

La Lista de Control para Esposos Gay
Y Para Mujeres Que se Preguntan

Spanish edition of
The Gay Husband Checklist for Women Who Wonder

Note from the Author

This book was first written in 2004. It has been nearly ten years since the original writing. Other than updating some of my own personal information, almost everything else has remained the same. I believe that the feelings and sentiments expressed here are the same as they were when this was written.

SPECIAL THANKS TO MAUREEN TILLMAN

I would like to give special thanks to Maureen Tillman, a very special friend, extraordinary artist, and a member of my straight wives support network, who created the cover for this updated version of *Doomed Grooms*. Maureen also designed the cover for *Straight Wives Shattered Lives Volume 2*. Her beautiful healing artwork can be viewed and purchased on her Etsy website. Here is her information:

http://MaureenTillman.etsy.com

Maureen's blog can be seen at:
http://MaureenTillman.blogspot.com

Contents

Introduction

In 2000, I published the book, **"The Gay Husband Checklist for Women Who Wonder."** It was a self-help book for women who wanted to understand about the dynamics of gay men who marry straight women without revealing their homosexuality. I found myself in this position in the early 1980's, and after the end of my marriage, I started a national support movement to help women understand how these marriages come about.

I know that after I discovered my own husband's homosexuality, I felt isolated, frightened and embarrassed thinking that I was the only woman who was ever in this situation. Thirty years ago, straight/gay marriages were virtually closeted and there was very limited information about them. Also, the Internet had yet to be developed as a vehicle of mass communication as it is today. I learned through years of personal research that there are millions of women struggling through this disaster. It was my intent to enlighten them about my own experiences in hopes that they could realize they were not alone or responsible for causing or creating homosexuality in their husbands.

I began doing television, radio, and newspaper interviews throughout the 1980's as my own philosophies and understanding about straight/gay marriages developed and changed. I was trying to bring national awareness to this issue in order to reach those women who felt there was no hope for future happiness in their lives because they were stuck in a disastrous marriage. Four years later, after working with over 5,000 women, I went into a semi-retirement. My own children were growing up and I wanted to spare them further hurt from a world that was extremely homophobic with the panic from AIDS. I also needed a break in the action so I could move on with my own personal life. Listening to the disheartening stories of women day in and day out seemed to give me a jaded view on relationships in general, leaving me feeling paralyzed to move ahead in my own personal life. I continued to do some limited private counseling, but I made a conscientious effort to focus on additional areas of my career.

When my children grew into adulthood, I decided to return to my writing and counseling knowing that there were still millions of women living the same life of despair as those 20 years earlier. Even though our country became less obsessed with the homophobic hysteria of the 1980's, the lack of acceptance for homosexuals was still a reality. Gays were still discriminated against and taunted which really is the bottom line of why they feel compelled to marry straight women in hopes that "straight" will be acquired through sexual transmission. There was still limited information available for a large group of people who were being affected by these marriages. A handful of books were available for resources, but so much more needed to be said.

I wanted to write a book that was clear and easy to understand. I wanted to give direct answers to complex questions. I wanted to show how these marriages came about, and more importantly, I wanted to show why they needed to end as quickly as possible.

Since launching my website in 1998 and publishing the book in 2000, I have received tens of thousands of letters from women and men who are trying to make sense of their complicated lives. Those who read my first book **"The Gay Husband Checklist for Women Who Wonder"** feel that for the first time, they can understand why their marriages have been so debilitating and what steps they need to take for their futures. It has been so rewarding for me to be able to help women make their first steps in understanding that the problems in their marriages are not their issues, but rather homosexuality. And from the several thousand gay men who have asked me for help, I have been able to give them the guidance and support to be honest with their wives, no matter what the consequences may be.

Although I have worked with thousands of women since 1984 when I started my counseling and support group, the last few years since my website and book emerged brought me thousands of new stories from women around the world who are suffering through these marriages or the aftermath. Their stories have compelled me to write this follow-up because so many additional issues needed to be addressed. Some of these concerns were touched on in my first book, but they required a much more comprehensive discussion. This book will cover the most important issues in a way that will guide women through the process of understanding, accepting, and moving forward in their lives.

Gays Can Change, Can't They?

When women first discover that the man they married is gay, they go through a period of denial. This is the first step in the mourning process when the death of your marriage is looming over you. It doesn't seem to matter whether the husband comes out to his wife or she discovers the news on her own. It doesn't matter if the signs have been there for years or if the wife saw no hint at all. The reaction is usually the same. "This can't be happening. How could my husband be gay? He married me. He made love to me. He created children with me. How can he be gay?"

The problem is that even in this day and age, **we don't understand gay**. We are much more familiar with homosexuality today than several decades ago when I married my gay husband. Gay is no longer a closeted issue. We see **gay** in television and movies, read about it in magazines and books, and listen to it on the radio. We all know gay people because of those who are leading an openly gay life and are not ashamed to say it. We know gay people through school, work, or recreational activities. We believe we have a handle on the whole gay thing. Gay means people who have same sex attractions and relationships, right?

Wrong. The gay that we see is the "identifiable gay" that we have been taught to be tolerant and accepting of. It is not uncommon to hear women say, "Some of my closest friends are gay," specifically referring to gay men. Straight women love gay men because they have a certain charm and sensitivity that straight men seem to lack. Many women I counseled have commented that they had gay male friends whom they socialized with and some even went to gay bars with these friends. They always felt comfortable with their gay male friends.

4

That's why it's inconceivable that they married a gay man. They were so sure they knew what gay was.

And how is it if they are so accepting of these gay male friends, it is suddenly a new ball game when they discover their husbands are gay? Why is it that "gay" now becomes the enemy? Quite simple—*having a gay friend is vastly different than having a gay husband.* We can accept gay in friendships, but we cannot accept gay in our marriages. And that is okay. ***Gay does not belong in a marriage to a straight woman.***

No normal thinking woman wants to think that her husband is out there having sex with other men or getting sexually aroused by the sight of two men having sex while looking at gay pornography. It's humiliating and debilitating to any woman's sense of self-esteem. And that's why so many women in the Initial grieving stage of *denial* believe that whatever it is that their husbands are feeling is merely a stage or phase that he is passing through.

Some women start looking for rational reasons: *"My husband must be bi-curious. All men go through this stage." "It doesn't mean anything just because he's visiting gay websites. He says it's funny." "The only thing he does is look at gay pornography. He swears he would never act on it. He thinks it's forbidden fruit and that turns him on."*

I've heard some of the most incredible rationalizations over the years as to why a gay man can't possibly be gay. And I understand the desperation that women go through trying to make excuses or find justification to the worst possible scenario any wife can envision.

Although I try to be gentle and compassionate when responding to these calls for help, I am honest with anyone who asks me for the answers. What I find is that women aren't necessarily looking for the truth—*they are asking me to perform a miracle.* They are convinced that I have some magical solution to changing their husbands. They turn to me hoping that I can give them encouragement and hope. They want me to tell them how to make their husbands' attractions to men disappear. They are desperate to find a way to make the problem go away.

Often they feel hurt, disappointment, and even anger when I tell them that their husbands won't and can't change. Well, maybe their behaviors can change for a while, but ultimately, they can't change their sexuality. No matter how these women try to "fix" themselves, the problem is they are not broken. They are women. Their husbands want men.

Some women challenge me. "I don't care what other couples have gone through—we will be the exception. We will be the couple that is able to make it because we love each other so much. We are both determined to keep our marriage together. My husband loves me enough that he is willing to resist all homosexual urges when they come his way. We both agree that as long as he is honest and communicates when this happens, we can work it through."

I always wish these women and their gay husbands good luck. Who am I to argue about supernatural abilities? We live in an age of miracles, and you just never know when one is going to happen. I keep an open mind even if it has doubtful thoughts. I never close the door on someone who is that filled with optimism and determination. I know that someday they will need to reopen it again, and I never want them to feel that pride has to come before the fall. I always end my responses back to them with sincere words of good luck and the parting words of, "If you ever need me, know that I am always here for you."

When they write to me months or years later humbling themselves, I **never** say, "I told you so." I hate that. Some people just need time to find out for themselves that this is not a livable situation. As much as their husbands try to make those urges go away, and as much as they "communicate" the problem to death, it is still there. Sometimes the urges are stronger than ever because now they are working harder than ever to not have them. That's when the resentment starts taking shape in full force. Now the wife, who was the most important person in his life, becomes his enemy.

The gay husband who was previously willing to do almost anything to keep the marriage in tact now starts thinking differently. "Why can't you just let me be who I am? Why are you trying to turn me into someone I can't be?" They were willing to compromise, but now they don't feel that they are "compromising" any more. Now they think they are giving up everything. And whose fault is it? Well, it's your fault—of course. You are the one forcing all of these feelings of frustration and suppression. You are the one making your husband conform to your rules. It's really a lose-lose situation, but it's one that both parties have to realize that they are losing before any changes can be made.

Some wives will try the road to compromise as an necessary evil. That's where the boundaries of your agreements start stretching. "Okay, if you go out once in a while and I never have to know about it and you don't do anything except socialize with other gay men, I can live with it." Okay—give him an inch. Then you find out that he's taking a foot, and then a yard. Once in a blue moon becomes once every few months, then every few weeks, then every week, etc. You know the drill.

What hurts the reality check most of all is when zealous religious or right wing groups come out with studies claiming that gays can change. In this century, you wouldn't think that anyone would even notice these studies anymore, but that's not the case. In the year 2001, a study came out that actually made the national news around the world stating that gays could change. The study was conducted by a professor from Columbia University, giving it credibility in the eyes of even those who sit on the fence not sure whether or not homosexuality is really a choice or not. The study said that a combination of therapy and religion can change a person's sexual orientation. This study was conducted on a number of gay people who were very desperate to change their sexual orientation and some were successful in "becoming" straight—or at least in leading a straight life.

Did this study surprise me? Not at all. Many groups and individuals have been trying to change gay to straight for years. In the past, there were all kinds of aversion therapy methods used such as electric shocks when gay men became aroused by watching pictures of other males in hopes of changing their brain patterns. There are numerous religious support groups that help gay men "become" straight. I've seen and heard it all. What surprised me is that a professor at Columbia University was viewed as if he had some magical approach that hasn't been tried before. It's news like this that sets back the whole problem by years. Instead of acknowledging that gay people are born as gay people and deserve to live their lives as gay people, now there is once again false hope that if you mentally obliterate homosexuality from the mindset it will disappear.

Ironically, the month that my book **"The Gay Husband Checklist for Women Who Wonder"** was released in May 2000, another book was also released the same month--**"Coming Out Straight"** by Richard Cohen. I discovered it accidentally when I went into Amazon.com to check if my book was listed as available yet. When I typed in the key words, my book did not come up because it would take two more weeks for it to be listed. What did appear was "Coming Out Straight." Now, normally I would have just exited the site and tried again a few days later. But when I saw the author was Richard Cohen, my heart skipped a beat or two and I stared in shock.

I am sure that Richard Cohen did not know that my book had just been published. What was so ironic was the fact that I had written about him in that book. I had several pages about Richard, my best friend during my late teenage years, regarding his struggle with homosexuality. I used him as an example of how people could change their sexuality through brainwashing. Richard was an active member and leader (even if it was low-level) in a cult movement known by the public as "Moonies" led by a Korean minister, Reverend Sun Myung Moon in the 1970's. This was during a period of my life when I was a political activist in New York City. For those of you who are too young to remember this group, the Moonies was the largest of cult groups during the 1970's. It ripped families apart by not allowing them near their brainwashed Moonie family members. These were the sleep-deprived people selling flowers in the streets and airports to raise money to keep their leader in great prosperity.

In my book, I tell the story of my friendship with Richard in high school. He was a year younger than me, but we were best of friends while I was in 11th and 12th grade. Richard was one of the most popular guys in school. Women fell for him easily because he was handsome, charming, funny, and personable. Back in the late 1960's, we were really in the dark about homosexuality. People would kid about it, but no one was fessin' up to it, especially in high school. To be labeled "queer" back in those days was a death sentence to any possible social life or friendships that you had. It was not an option back then. If you had these feelings, you needed to suppress and hide them so deeply that no one would suspect. You didn't even dare to suspect yourself because the reality was far too painful to think about.

As Richard's friend, I gained a new sense of popularity and friendship from young ladies who felt I could help them in their quest to get Richard as a boyfriend. It was one of the perks of being his friend. Richard did have several long-term relationships with high school girls that ended as he went to college.

One of the vivid memories I described was an attempted sexual encounter that Richard and I tried one night. We were drinking a bottle of wine and started to feel giddy. One thing led to another. We began kissing and touching each other, planning to go wherever the mood took us. It didn't take us anywhere, and I think we were both relieved about that. We were best friends and that might have put a crimp in the friendship.

One evening when I was 18 and he was 17, we went to New York and spent the night there in a hotel room. We slept in the same bed—strictly as friends. As we walked through the city streets, I kept pointing out to Richard guys who I thought were handsome. He revealed to me several years later when he came out to me that on that night, he was checking out whether our taste in men was the same or different. He knew what he was as a teenager, but he was hoping that those feelings would go away.

When Richard entered college and moved several states away, he came back during one of his semester breaks in his junior year and told me that he needed to speak to me about something important. I had my own apartment in Philadelphia and invited him to come over for coffee. It's funny how some incidents seem important enough to remember so many years later because of their shock value at the time the words are said. That's when Richard told me that he was gay. He told me he finally understood where he fit in and he was not ashamed to be gay. When I questioned him about his past relationships with women, he told me that it just never felt right. I was still somewhat naïve and didn't exactly understand homosexuality, but I accepted it and wished him the best of luck with his new lifestyle. I had just returned from nearly two years in California where gay was open and I had made gay friends. And that was it. I didn't see him or hear from him again until seven years later when I accidentally passed him on 34th Street in New York City.

I've seen this scene in movies where two people who haven't seen each other for years pass each other on the street, turn around, run to each other in excitement and embrace. I felt on that day my life was like a movie. Richard was walking towards 7th Avenue, and I was walking towards 6th Avenue. I passed him, took a few seconds to filter the face, turned around at the same moment he did, and ran to each other and embraced. Who could believe that my best high school friend was here in New York City walking on the same street I was walking at the same moment after all of those years? We were jumping up and down holding each other. When we calmed down, I asked him why he was in New York

At first, he didn't want to tell me. He said that he was following my activist career, and he knew that I wouldn't approve of his activities. I couldn't imagine what he meant by that. I assured him that there was nothing that would cause me to care any less about him. He still didn't want to tell me. It then struck me—he was heading toward a building on the next block that was the headquarters for Reverend Moon. I asked him if he was part of the group, and he hesitantly said, "Yes." Then I understood why he didn't want to tell me. The Moonies was one of the groups that my organization was fighting against. In fact, we were involved with people who used to whisk up their members upon the begging of hysterical parents and help send them on their way for deprogramming. It hurt me to think that my high school best friend had been sucked into this movement.

I promised to put our political differences to the side. Nothing was more important than our past strong bond of friendship. Unfortunately, Richard didn't have those kinds of choices he could make. After two visits, he was ordered not to have any further contact with me. When I went to the building to visit him, I was told not to try to reach him again. I knew not to push my luck because this group could be dangerous, and life went on.

The most interesting part of our conversation on the day we met was when Richard told me he was getting married to a Korean woman. I was shocked. I asked him how this could happen since he was gay. He felt very good about the fact that he was no longer gay. When I questioned that, he told me that thanks to Reverend Moon, he was able to overcome that part of his life. Now he was about to embark on marriage with a woman on her way to this country. I was amazed by this change, but I also knew how powerful brainwashing could be. If Reverend Moon was able to get people to give up their families, homes, and life savings, then giving up their homosexuality was probably a piece of cake. I saw Richard several days later for the last time before becoming barred from entering the building he lived in by the security guards.

I next heard about Richard in the early 1990's when the ABC show 20/20 advertised an upcoming segment on how homosexuals can change. The promotion showed a picture of

Richard with his Korean wife and children. It was somewhat more difficult to fool me by then. I was divorced from my own gay husband and had been counseling straight/gay couples for nearly 10 years. I knew better than to think someone could flip back and forth with his sexuality like a remote control.

I felt sure that when Richard revealed how Reverend Moon changed his life, they would see through the façade, and he would have no credibility. I was in for a surprise as I watched that segment. He never mentioned anything about Reverend Moon. He only stated that through prayer, anyone could change. His proof was his wife and their children, who also appeared on the program.

I was really angry after the show. I called the producers of 20/20 and told them that they didn't do their homework on this man. They never mentioned about his "brainwashing" by Reverend Moon or that he was ever part of a powerful cult group and arranged marriage. They told me to write a letter to the producer, but since the segment had aired, there was nothing they could do. I wrote my letter stating my accusations, but no response was ever received.

I didn't hear anything more about Richard Cohen until the fateful day that I checked out Amazon.com. When I read the review about his book and his ministry to help gay people with "reorientation" into heterosexuality, I found it chilling. And, his review proudly announced that Dr. Laura Schlessinger, one of America's top experts in "family unity," wrote the introduction. Dr. Laura was raised with a religious Jewish background, so I was so sure that she was duped when agreeing to write this introduction for a former leader of the Moonie group.

I ordered the book so I could see for myself what Richard wrote about his "reorientation" back to heterosexuality and his ties to Reverend Moon. I was sure that even though it was omitted on the 20/20 segment, it would be revealed in his book and his own personal life story.

When I did read his book, I was disappointed that there was no mention of Reverend Moon at all. He did refer to the

Unification Church in several places, but to most people today, this doesn't mean anything. In fact, it is easy to confuse this as meaning the Unitarian Church, which is in no way related other than by the first few letters that start the words. And so Richard's book looked innocent enough to those who didn't know the real story. First he found Jesus, then he re-found heterosexuality. Nowhere does he mention that Reverend Moon was the catalyst in his conversion to whatever form of Christianity the Unification Church cult movement embraces.

Richard boasts about "returning" numerous gay men back to their "heterosexual" birthright. He believes that all men are born straight. They just get screwed up somewhere along the way and become gay. It's just a matter of finding what that screw up is and untangling it back to its original form. He believes in most cases, as in his life, it's due to the lack of positive father-son relationships in childhood and adolescence. It does take some work, but eventually, through Jesus and Richard Cohen, you can be free of your homosexual shackles.

Someone like this might have impressed me a bit more if only he was honest. Let me clarify that. His cause would never impress me because I think it's disgraceful to try to change gay people into being straight. It's even worse than those people tampering with genetics so they can someday clone people into whatever size and shape is popular. It's worse because the people experimenting with genetics are working on the unborn. Richard Cohen is working on people who are alive and thinking human beings. They are vulnerable and confused. They are internally suffering from all of the external messages they hear about homosexuality. And this message makes them think that rather than accept yourself for who you are, here's something even better—you can be someone who you're not--*if only you try hard enough.*

Getting back to impressing me—I may have been impressed if he was honest about his relationship with Reverend Moon because people would then understand how his thinking was truly influenced, namely through brainwashing. But instead, when I put out a national press release exposing his background shortly after our books came out, his supporters sent me a barrage of email telling me that there was no way he could have been a leader in the Moon movement. They came up with reasons such as "he isn't Korean", "he had no real power," and "he was only briefly in the movement." They really were looking to stretch a point here with semantics.

I did research his role in the movement in case my memory from 20 years earlier was on overload. I found at least three speeches given by Reverend Moon where he mentioned Richard by name. He wasn't just another innocent face selling flowers on the street. He was part of his public relations team spreading the word to those lost souls who were willing to listen.

Richard's supporters claimed he broke away from the church in recent years because it just wouldn't give him the support he was looking for. Whatever that means. It's irrelevant to me. I know where his background and thinking come from. It's very hard to break away from something that is so engrained in your psyche. It is a mental pull that is so strong that it can actually change the ways of your sexuality. That's what mind alteration can do to someone. Certainly it happened to Richard Cohen no matter what he chooses to state publicly.

The claims of Richard Cohen and others like him are dangerous because it keeps the fires of homophobia burning. It gives critics of homosexuality fuel because it feeds into their theory that homosexuality is a choice that can be "unchosen" if someone wants it badly enough, or in Cohen's case, straightens out the dysfunction in his own family. It sends out a clear message stating that our husbands can *choose* to be straight if they really want to be straight. Ergo, if men refuse to take the necessary steps for change, it's because they really don't want to. They have made the "*choice*" to stay gay. They don't love their wives or families enough to do the right thing.

For those of us living this life, we know this is not true. Even if men can suppress their sexual needs and not act of them, it doesn't mean that they are happy doing this. The frustration that

14

sets in is taken out on the wives who can't understand why they can't make their husbands happy. Eventually this unhappiness turns to resentment and emotional abuse towards the wife for keeping the man in a place where he doesn't belong and doesn't want to be.

If anyone should change, it needs to be the wife. She needs to change her determination to have her husband stay in the marriage and be straight when he is gay. And guess what? It's much easier to have this mental change come about than the physical sexuality change of a husband. It's not easy, but it's possible. People recover all of the time from broken hearts and broken marriages. This is human. But to expect a man to change his genetic makeup is inhuman. It's unnatural. It's also unfair—to both of you.

Why is it unfair? **Because marriage was never meant to be this complicated or challenging.** Trust me. Homosexuality is one of those "unforeseen" events in life that is thrown into a crapshoot. And like any other gamble, sometimes you have to know when to cut your losses. You can spend wasted years of your life trying to make something work when it is not workable. You can wake up every day in a state of existence because *you* choose to stay in a marriage with a man who cannot be the husband you need. You can make a choice to change so much more easily than your gay husband, and yet you expect that he can make an impossible choice when you can't make a logical one.

Don't get me wrong. I know and understand desperation. I understand the fear of being alone and starting over. I have faced the demon called loneliness and have had it embrace me causing me to shed tears up to my ankles. But I have survived it and come out all that much stronger.

I could have stayed with my gay husband in our *doomed* marriage. Even though he walked out on me on that fateful September day in 1982, he came back a week later, suitcase in hand waiting for me to admit defeat. But in that one week, my inner strength returned allowing me to say the words, "I'm not taking you back." And even though I knew I had to say them, I was hurting badly. I was scared—petrified is actually more accurate. And yet there was a survival instinct that roared inside me that day that allowed those words to come out of my mouth.

I was very vulnerable at that point. I had a two-and-a-half year old daughter who gave new meaning to the term "terrible two's." I also had a three-month-old son who had been in the hospital a half-dozen times since his birth for a chronic illness that had yet to be diagnosed. I was penniless because our business had gone down the drain leaving us with only debts and angry workers knocking on my door to get their pay that I didn't have. I had no phone, no car, and just a few dollars left from the original $50.00 my husband had left on the table when he walked out a week earlier. It would have been very easy to say, "Okay, you can come back now and I will give in to your terms." But I didn't. I couldn't. I was dying inside either way. The difference was the method of death. One way would be a torturous death. That's the one where I'd allow my husband to return home so he would continue to emotionally strip away whatever little sanity I had left. The other way was a quiet, dignified death where I stood a chance of reviving from my own personal "code blue." And so I took my chances and picked what seemed to be the harder way out, but the best chance at long-term survival and "revival."

Ending my marriage was the best thing I could have done— for both of us and our children. Living in a hostile environment is not conducive to successful childrearing. My daughter had spent much of her first two-and-a-half years in the middle of a war zone and it took its effect. She was nervous and high strung. We showed her plenty of love, but the screaming and angry behavior on a progressive basis left its scars.

My ex-husband needed a chance to have a life where he didn't have to keep living a lie. To stay married to me would have forced him to be someone who he wasn't. I needed a chance to find myself and become a person who could fulfill her potential rather than live in the shadows of my husband's dark secretive side, calculating daily how I was going to trap him or trick him into telling me the truth. This was marriage at its worst, and it needed to end.

I work with so many women whose marriages need to end, and yet they continue to stay in it year after year after year. When I think about all of the wasted time that women are spending in these marriages, it makes me very sad. These are years that lack affection, passion, compassion, and intimacy. These are years that drain away their sense of self-esteem and self-worth. These are years when these women are forced into celibacy exile because their husbands will not have sex with them. For many, it is years of stunted growth because without nurturing, people don't grow to reach their potential. It's like watering flowers so they can bloom. These are years filled with frustration, anger, self-blame, and tears. **This is not the way life was meant to be.**

I never judge women who write me about their pain. I am a patient woman. I know how difficult it is to walk away from a mudslide—or more like a pool of quicksand. Every woman has to move at her own pace. And as long as a woman recognizes that there is a problem in her marriage, there is hope. As long as a woman knows that she is unhappy because she is living with a gay husband, there is a chance of changing it. I have worked with the most shattered and battered of women who felt there was no way out short of death. But with enough support, encouragement, and logical thinking, they have realized that there are positive choices they can make—and in time, they make them.

To all the women who write to me about going to marriage counseling to save their marriages, I extend the same advice. Same your time and save your money. Any marriage counselor who will take your business to try to "save" your marriage after knowing that your husband is gay is robbing you. Your marriage ultimately won't be saved because gay men are not meant to be in straight marriages. If you want to go for counseling, go yourself and build up your strength to find your independence so you can move on. Then find support through friends, families, women's groups, divorce groups, etc. and start the process. The bottom line is, "Gays can't change," but you can!

The Internet

I admit it. I was way behind the times. I was so computer resistant and computer illiterate until the mid 1990's. I took the attitude that if I were meant to learn the computer, I would have been born twenty years earlier. Living in a world of ignorance was bliss, I suppose. I had no idea what new worlds of information would open to me once I was introduced to the Internet several years ago.

Once I launched my own website on the Internet, the mail started coming in. Many of the letters were from straight wives of gay men who were blaming the Internet for being the *cause* of their husbands' homosexuality. Their husbands would tell them that they had no idea they were gay until they started visiting gay websites. And then *Voila*! They were transformed from being (what these wives usually describe in their words as) loyal, dedicated straight husbands into unconscionable "gay" husbands as if the click of a mouse created the "sexuality preference change."

While it's true that the Internet did give men access to gay websites, it certainly didn't "turn" them gay. Nor would the Internet be able to take a curious straight man and turn him into a homosexual just by looking at a gay website. Nor would a straight man keep revisiting a gay Internet site out of curiosity. Once yes—more than that--**no.**

What the Internet did was give gay men who were hiding or "passing" in straight marriages the opportunity to explore their homosexuality without leaving home. These were often men who were too afraid to *think* these feelings and just lived harboring them inside in hopes they would pass or go away. They were men who could be found sneaking into an adult book store and anonymously buying gay pornography only having to find a suitable hiding place where their wives couldn't find it. Or they would find themselves glancing at men and fantasizing because they feared the reality of their fantasies.

Now, armed with mouse in hand, they were able to find anything they wanted on the Internet including hook-up websites, pornography, chatrooms, magazines, stories, and personals. For many of these men, it became an addiction. They would sit for hours on the computer entering a world that they previously didn't have access to without blowing their cover. They never had to leave their computer chair to be taken to a sexual Shangri-La beyond their imagination.

They started out so carefully, but some of them became careless in time. They were so obsessed with the computer that they unintentionally left evidence for their wives to find. And when their wives would find it and confront them, they came up with explanations worthy of mention. They included, *"All men look at gay porno. It's a source of entertainment and makes me laugh,"* to *"I am helping my friend at work. He thinks he's gay and he doesn't have a computer. He asked me to do some research for him,"* to *"Someone must have come into the house and used our computer. There's no other way to explain it."*

At first, women want to believe these explanations. They breathe a sign of relief and try hard to buy into the bizarre. Even the alleged "mysterious stranger" who visits the home to use the computer to access gay websites seems to be easier to digest than the actual reality of your husband being gay. And you may think, "How stupid could these women be to believe these stories?" Well, hindsight is always the best teacher.

Remember, the majority of women had no reason to think that their husbands were gay. There were no obvious signs, no visible clues. A few even thought they had the ideal marriage. Take, for instance, the story of Laura who first wrote to me in the spring of 2001. This is her story:

"Roy and I married in 1991. For almost ten years, we were the couple of envy among our friends. I felt like I was the luckiest woman in the world because I had the "perfect" marriage. I met my husband at a company party. We both worked for a large corporation in different parts of a large business complex. I never saw him before the party, even though we both had been working there for several years. He was charming, intelligent, attentive, and flirtatious. We just clicked. The chemistry was strong. Very rarely did a man impress me so quickly. He asked me for my phone number with a promise to call soon."

"I didn't hear from Roy for three weeks, and I couldn't understand how my instincts were so far off. When he did call with explanations about being called out of town for a business emergency, I was so happy. He seemed eager to see me and we made plans for dinner the next night."

"It was a fairy tale romance. I was 26 years old and had done my fair share of dating. I had two short-term relationships that didn't go anywhere because they lacked the excitement I felt with Roy. He was affectionate, always holding my hand, stroking my hair, and kissing me gently. Unlike other men who just wanted to get me from the living room to the bedroom, Roy was clear that he wasn't rushing me into bed because we had a lifetime to make love."

"Within the first few months, we both knew that this was the relationship we had been waiting for. Roy was three years older than me. He told me about a previous engagement that ended two weeks before the marriage when he found his fiancé in bed with another man. He was so devastated. He gave up on ever finding his true love, but then I appeared. At least that's the story he told me, and at the time, I had no reason to doubt him."

"I came from a religious Catholic family, and the fact that Roy wanted to wait to have sex until after the marriage was another important part of the picture. Most men were not so considerate of my personal beliefs. This made me love Roy that much more. There were times, I admit, when I was ready to make love, but Roy convinced me it would make the relationship that much more exciting and valid if we waited until after the wedding."

"We married ten months after we met, and all of my family and friends were there to wish us well. Roy had only his office friends because his childhood friends were over 2,000 miles away in the town where he grew up. He had only lived in Washington State for three years after a transfer from his hometown of Tennessee. He also told me early in the relationship that he didn't have any close family. He was an only child of parents that died in a car accident when he was eleven years old. He spent several years in a group home for orphans before being emancipated."

"Our honeymoon was wonderful. Although making love was a little awkward the first few times, it was gentle and caring. Our relationship as a couple was wonderful. Roy was an attentive husband, always complimenting me about my looks, housekeeping, and cooking, while making me feel good about myself. We both decided to start a family that year. Roy was anxious to have children because he grew up as an only child and felt isolated because he didn't have any family left of his own. I conceived during our second year of marriage, and nine months later, our daughter Sarah was born. Roy was a doting father, and our lives seemed so cemented together. Two years later, our son Justin was born. Now Roy bragged that we were the ideal American family."

"Roy and I developed a circle of wonderful friends. Some of the couples were from our company; some were new friends we made as our children became school age and developed friends; and some were from our church where we were active members. We regularly went on family outings, and every weekend was filled with friends."

"Over the years, some of our friends had marital problems. They always felt they could safely confide in Roy and me because they looked to us for guidance. They would ask us how we kept our marriage so happy. We explained to them that our marriage was strong because we had the key ingredients to building it—namely, trust, communication, and love."

"Communication was so important to us. We would talk about everything important and trivial. We would laugh together and cry together. Even when we didn't agree on something, we respected each other's different opinions. Arguments were so rare, and when they did occur, we were determined to follow that rule of "never go to bed angry." We made sure to talk everything out and resolve our differences before the lights were turned off."

"It's true that our sex life had diminished greatly over the ten years. This didn't seem to be too unusual in view of our extremely busy lives and the constant attention we gave the children. Many nights we found them sneaking into our bed, and because we loved them so much, we let them stay there. But the affection was always there. Roy was always wrapping his arms around me as we slept, and kissed me repeated times during the day. Not a day went by without his telling me that he loved me."

"During our eighth year of marriage, Roy received a promotion into an executive position with our company. I had reduced my hours to part-time after our son was born, so the extra income was a major boost. Roy knew that the position would force him to work extra hours and travel, but we both agreed it was a wonderful opportunity that couldn't be passed up. He worked hard over the years to get this promotion, and when the chance presented itself, he grabbed it."

"Some evenings Roy wouldn't get home until after 10:00 at night. He would practically fall through the door with exhaustion, kiss me, and fall asleep. He decided that we needed a computer at home so that he could work on some of his projects late at night rather than stay in the office. The company was willing to buy him one for use at home, and I thought that would make things easier. We converted a spare bedroom into a workroom and Roy set up his home office. He was very clear with the children and me that when the office door was closed, it was like he was at work. He was not to be disturbed because this would be time that he would have to spend away from home if he were at his company. Even though those work sessions could last for hours, it seemed logical in view of all of the new responsibilities that Roy acquired with his new job."

"There were also business trips that started that same year. Every few weeks, Roy would fly out of town for meetings. He usually returned within two or three days, and he always called us in the morning and at night to check on how we were doing. We had less time to spend with our friends because Roy was so busy with his new job. Now our friends started asking me if something was wrong with our marriage because they hardly saw us anymore. I assured them it was just the responsibility of the new position. I don't think that some of them believed me no matter how much I assured them that things were fine."

"I don't know what made me start thinking that maybe things weren't as fine as I kept telling everyone. Personally, I blamed the job, but Roy started to seem different. He was still loving and caring, but at times seemed distanced. When I would try to talk about it, he assured me it was just exhaustion and pressure. I offered to return to work full time in case he felt the job was too much. There was no shame in feeling overwhelmed if he wanted to rethink the new responsibilities. He felt so appreciative of my offer, but kindly refused, telling me that things would normalize in time. It's just that his department was expanding and it was a tribute to his ability for growing with the company."

"One weekend when Roy was away, I decided to use his computer. He was very clear that the computer was not for personal use since the company was paying for it. He warned me that the company metered the time on there because they paid the bills. They would be able to tell if it was being used for personal use because they would check the sites that were being visited. I didn't know very much about computers, and I accepted that explanation. But a friend of mine kept raving about a website that I was anxious to look up, so I thought I'd take a chance. A few minutes on the computer couldn't possibly mess things up that much, right?"

"I suppose that over the months Roy trusted that I would not use his computer so he didn't think to turn it off. When I went in, the computer was on and there was a screen with his email on there. At first, I just glanced as I looked for the box where I could type in the website. But my eyes were stuck on the email addresses I found on the screen. A number of the addresses had the word "gay" in them. My curiosity got the best of me and I started clicking into the mail. I wasn't prepared for what I found. There were advertisements for gay pornography. There were pictures of naked young men holding their private parts in their hand. There were letters from dozens of men who claimed they enjoyed chatting with Roy and had explicit sexual language in them. I became fixated on this mail and obsessively checked each letter. I went into his old mail, his history file, his file cabinet, and anything else I could find. I spent over four hours that evening searching and searching while my heart kept pounding and pounding and my eyes kept crying. "

"I found letters from men in different parts of the country where Roy went on business trips talking about the wonderful night they had with him and how they were awaiting his return. It was very clear why Roy was too exhausted for us to have a sex life. He was obviously too worn down from having a very active sex life outside the home—and with men. I was able to track these letters back for 15 months when he first received the computer. When I went into the computer file cabinet, he even had the letters filed into various categories by state."

"I actually started pinching my skin to see if I was dreaming and having a nightmare. I had lost track of time and for a moment, I felt as if I were someone else in my own body. It's a hard feeling to describe. I didn't know what to do next. I physically collapsed and fell asleep until the phone rang and woke me up. It was morning, and Roy was checking in to see how we were doing. I told him I wasn't feeling very well and he sounded worried. "Do you want me to come home? I can leave my business meeting now and fly back by this afternoon." I told him no, it was just a virus and I'd talk to him later. I needed time to process everything to decide what to do."

"I felt ashamed and embarrassed. I'm not sure why I felt that way; Roy should be the one to feel like that. But I did. I felt that a bullet had hit me in the gut and that I was dying. I mechanically made breakfast for the children and got them off to school. I called in sick to work because there was no way I'd be able to function. I kept thinking did other people in our company know? Were they thinking that I was stupid? Did I do something that made Roy turn to men for sex? Who could I turn to for information?"

"I knew Roy wasn't gay. He married me, made love to me, had two children with me, and told me every day how much he loved me. Why would he want to have sex with men? Gay men didn't marry women and have wonderful marriages like we did. I just didn't understand how this was happening. Where would I go to find out? Who could I turn to? I didn't dare tell my family because they loved Roy as if he were their own son. They were strict Catholics and might feel that I had done something to encourage this behavior. I kept looking to myself to figure out what I had done to make Roy act in this shameful and sinful manner. He was a wonderful man. We had a wonderful marriage. Something just wasn't registering."

"Roy called me three times that day to check how I was feeling. I told him I was nauseous and that was the truth. My head was pounding as fast as my heart was palpitating. With all this motion going on in my body, I felt paralyzed and unable to move. And so I just sat and thought. I tried to think of anything that could have given me a clue or a hint about Roy's bizarre behavior, but there was nothing. It's true our sex life had dwindled to practically nothing, but after so many years of marriage, it didn't seem to be that unnatural. It was always circumstances that stopped us from making love, but Roy didn't seem to complain or feel slighted. He never pushed for sex, but even if he felt he was missing it, would that make him turn to men? Why not women? Whenever the issue of homosexuality came up among our friends, he even seemed somewhat homophobic. He said it was "unnatural" and men didn't have to "choose" to be gay if they wanted to be straight. Some of our friends didn't agree with him, but no one could persuade him to change his mind."

"After thinking and thinking, I decided that whatever Roy was going through could be turned around if I tried harder to be his lover. I was also at fault for not pursuing our physical relationship. I had to put those ugly thoughts in the back of my head if there was a chance to reverse this tragedy. I decided that I was not going to tell Roy about what I found on the computer. I was going to "solve" the problem by being the kind of wife he needed in the bedroom."

"I was glad Roy would be away for another day so I could have time to compose myself. I was so afraid I was going to give away the secret I had learned. I sent the children to a friend's house for the night so we could spend some quiet time together. He arrived home late in the day armed with "get well" presents for me. I greeted him with our traditional hug and kiss and thanked him for his thoughtfulness. He asked for the children, but I told him I wanted this to be a special night for us. He couldn't understand why at first, but I explained that it had been so long since we had a whole night to ourselves, and we needed to "reconnect" so to speak."

"At first, he seemed a little hesitant. "Reconnect? In what way?" I explained that as a wife and husband, it had been a long time since we had been intimate. I prepared a special dinner for the occasion and ran out earlier in the day to buy a sexy nightgown to entice him for the evening. He told me that it would take him about a half hour to catch up on his email for the job, but then we would have the rest of the night together. Although I cringed at the thought of what he would be reading on the computer, I agreed to get dinner ready while he checked. I took the phone of the hook so we would not be interrupted and put on some romantic music while I finished preparing dinner."

"I don't know why, but it actually seemed strange while we sat down to the meal. Roy couldn't understand why I would go through all of this after all the years we had been together. I told him that I wanted the night to be perfect, much like the nights we had early in our marriage. He reluctantly went along with my plan as we shared a bottle of our favorite wine. He praised the dinner and we started talking and laughing as if it were the old days."

"After dinner, I asked him if he would join me in the bedroom. I wanted to change into the new nightgown and progress with my plan. Again, he said that he was waiting for an urgent email and would join me as soon as he checked his messages. Then the night would be ours. I was mildly annoyed, but said okay so I would have time to transform myself. When he returned to the bedroom a few minutes later, I was waiting there with lit candles and my new lingerie. Roy said how beautiful I looked, and he slowly began taking off his clothes down to his underwear. He laid down in the bed and I started to message his back. He was always turned on by messaging in the past."

"I noticed there was hesitation in his making a move as I kept my hands moving up and down his back. I turned around to him and started kissing him the way we used to start our lovemaking. He responded, but there was a coldness in his lips. He started touching and caressing me, and I felt that feeling of warmth building in me. Unfortunately, it wasn't building in him. No matter how much I tried touching him, feeling him, and caressing him, there was nothing happening where it counts if you know what I mean. After nearly an hour of trying, we stopped. He kept saying he was sorry and claimed it was the exhaustion from the trip that was at fault. I was perfect he said, but he wasn't "functioning" right. I reassured him it was fine, although there were tears swelling up in my eyes. He promised we'd have a chance to make up for it very soon, and held me while I fell asleep."

"I was barely asleep when I felt him moving away from me ever so carefully so I wouldn't notice that he was getting up. He left the room and headed for his computer. He didn't have to say where he was going—I knew. I pretended to be asleep when he re-entered the bedroom nearly two hours later, and eventually I fell into an uncomfortable sleep. When I woke up, he was gone. He left me a note on the table thanking me for the wonderful evening the night before. He said that he loved me so much for trying to make the night special for him."

"I immediately went to his computer to see what activity had gone on after he left the bedroom. I went to his sent mail and found a lengthy email written to someone named Marc. To paraphrase to the best of my memory, it said, "Dear Marc, This has been a torturous evening at home. Laura suddenly decided it was time for us to have a romantic evening. You can imagine how that made me feel after the evening you and I spent together last night. She had everything waiting for me from dinner and wine to a new sexy nightgown. I really tried to accommodate (and I remember that word very vividly) her needs, but I couldn't do it. Every time I tried, I kept thinking of you and how excited I was to be in your arms. I tried to fantasize that Laura was you, but that was even more of a joke. I finally told her that I was just too exhausted. Whew, I hope she bought that story. And I hope that she gets that idea out of her head. I told you that I love Laura because she is a wonderful woman. But she can never do for me what you do for me.""

"It then went on to discuss some intimate details of their night before that I won't mention."

"After reading this letter, I went to the bathroom and threw up. I was literally sick. I felt as if I had been such an idiot. He was discussing our personal moments with a total stranger—at least he was a stranger to me. Obviously, not a stranger to him. I felt like screaming my lungs out, but I didn't know who to scream to so I just cried and cried. I think that was the shock I needed to make me understand that my marriage was over. I didn't understand how or why this happened, but I knew I was going to have to deal with it. I just needed to figure out how to proceed."

"I admit I was scared to death. In less than 72 hours, I moved from being the happiest woman married to feeling like the biggest fool in the world. My whole life was shattering in front of me. I never thought about being on my own. I believed that marriage was forever, and I wasn't mentally prepared to walk away on that particular day. Maybe Marc and I needed marriage counseling. Perhaps that would be the answer to his problem. He might be confused or mixed up. Maybe not having sex with him very often over the past few years threw him into some obscene world where sex was easy to get. I didn't really know what to think, but I wasn't willing to throw ten years down the drain without a fight. I may have lost the battle the night before, but I wasn't willing to lose the war."

"Without revealing why I was requesting marriage counseling, I suggested to Marc that night that we should consider getting some help for our marriage. He couldn't understand why I would feel that way, and, in fact, seemed hurt that his failure in bed would make me think that our marriage was in need of fixing. I tried to reassure him it was not the failure of the night before that prompted my suggestion. I told him I felt as if we were drifting apart and I wanted to refocus us as a couple. He felt that maybe I needed counseling without him because he was happy in our marriage. He didn't feel we had a problem—I did. But finally, he agreed to go because he wanted to prove "how much he loved me.""

"Over the next week, I asked some very close friends who had gone for marriage counseling for some guidance. They recommended a therapist they used and thought was very helpful. I thought it was odd that they didn't think that there was anything unusual for me to be making this request. Maybe they were able to pick up on something where I was blinded. I called Dr. Marlin and made an appointment for us to begin two weeks later. When I told Roy about the appointment, he said, "Okay, if that's what you want." I decided not to check his computer until after the appointment. I just was too afraid to look anymore."

"Our first session together was kind of ridiculous. I should have thought about it before I went. How could we both possibly get fair counseling if neither one of us was willing to be totally honest with the therapist? We each told the therapist about ourselves and gave a brief history of our nearly ten years together. When we were asked to state what we felt the problems in our marriage were, Roy said he would let me articulate the problems because he could not figure out yet that we had a problem. I said that I felt our communication had broken down. When the therapist asked me how, I just said that I felt we were drifting in separate directions. Roy and I both stated we loved each other, but I said the love seemed different now than before. I didn't exactly know how to explain how it was different without revealing what I knew."

"We left the session and made an appointment to return the following week. On our way home, Roy announced that he had no intention of going back for a second session. He claimed it was a waste of time and money. He suggested that I might need some therapy for myself if I was feeling unhappy. He even suggested that maybe I need some kind of "anti-depressant" if I'm feeling sad to put me into a better state of mind. I believe he meant a "numbing state of mind." I knew that when we reached our home, he would march to the computer and do the unthinkable. I didn't argue with him because it would go nowhere. "

"The next morning, as soon as Roy left for work, I checked his computer and looked at his emails that I had missed over the past two weeks. I forced myself to keep reading even though each one just made me sicker by the moment. I wasn't sure what to do at this point, but my survival instincts told me to start printing out as much of this garbage as possible. I spent the next few hours cutting and pasting emails together and then spent another hour or so printing out the "evidence" that I had a feeling I would need at some future time."

"Over the next several months, things just started sliding downhill at an accelerated rate. Roy would come home later and later, and a few nights, he called that he was too busy at work to come home at all. It's funny, but each day I started to care less and less if he was there. I was kind of relieved when he wasn't. It was getting harder each day to keep pretending that anything was all right when nothing was. He even stopped saying, "I love you," or giving me a kiss goodbye. Perhaps he sensed my distancing or was just at a point where he didn't care.

Ironically, he must have suspected something because one morning when I went through my new ritual of checking the computer, everything was missing. All records had been erased. His file cabinet had been emptied. And two days later, in order to get into his email, the computer told me that I needed a password, which previously had been stored to get me there automatically when I turned the computer on. I knew that I would never be able to find out future information like I had been doing. At that moment, I felt so grateful that I had printed out so much of his stuff and carefully hid it away where he would never find it."

This was the time when Laura started looking for support and information. She contacted me with her story, and after working together, she was able to understand that Roy's behavior had nothing to do with her. She was not the cause of the failure of her marriage, but rather homosexuality. Within a few weeks of Laura's contacting me, she confronted Roy with her evidence and demanded an explanation. He wasn't shocked at all like she anticipated. He had suspected that she was checking the computer and finding his information. That's why he had erased everything and added a password.

Roy said he was willing to stay married to Laura for the sake of keeping the family together, but she was strong enough at that point to say "No." She was not able to put the betrayal out of her head long enough to even consider that offer. Roy moved out in June of 2001, almost 10 years to the day of their marriage. In the months that followed, he rarely called or visited with the children. Laura quit her job and found a full-time position with another company to avoid running in to him at work. She also suspected that some of her co-workers were aware of Roy's activities by comments they had made. She felt too embarrassed to see people looking at her with either pity or silent accusations of stupidity.

Laura is having a difficult time juggling her new full-time job and being primarily a single parent with little and infrequent support from Roy. She has filed for a divorce, and he has agreed to it. They have had some legal complications over financial matters because this "good and loving" husband now doesn't continue to be quite as good or loving now that he is on his own. Hopefully in time, he'll reconnect to his family in a responsible way emotionally and financially and realize that he still has commitments to them.

So many women have been able to confirm their suspicions by accessing their husbands' computer activities. In the spring of 2001, I added a menu choice to my website called *"Catch Him."* Here I give women instructions on how to check the temporary Internet files on their computer. It is a wonderful thing for me to give easy instructions for the basically computer illiterates (like me!) to find those files and start looking for any suspicious ones that have "gay" in the titles. Within the first year, I had over 3,500 requests for these directions. Some of the letters I received afterwards were really heartbreaking. Women were finally able to understand what was wrong in their marriages. Even though some of the letters showed confusion, the proof was now very clear—at least to me, that is. Today you can buy spyware for under $100.00 that will track your husband on the computer if you have access to the computer he is using one time. You can monitor his emails, websites, instant messages, and files anytime from any computer--you don't have to do it from home.

Some women refuse to believe that their husbands are gay even with this evidence. These are the women who confronted their husbands with their findings and were assured that their suspicions were ridiculous. These are the husbands who came up with some of those excuses I discuss earlier in this chapter.

On a rare occasion, a husband would confess to the truth. But most stay in denial—at least to their wives. And some of their wives want to believe these denials so much that they accept the explanations. There's no accounting for the depths of desperation we all go to not to have to face the inevitable.

The bottom line—homosexuality was not caused by the Internet. It was only a matter of time before your husbands would find some other way to express their sexuality. The computer may be a vehicle as far as speeding up the inevitable, but the situation is what it is. One thing is for sure—your husband's homosexuality was in place long before technology helped him explore it.

Sexuality – Namely, Yours!

One of the most difficult subjects for wives of gay men to discuss is sexuality. I think the reason that we don't speak about it too often is because so many of us are sexually mutated or dead during and after our marriages. We have lost our sexual esteem by being made to feel as if we are aggressive, oversexed nymphomaniacs who can never be satisfied or fulfilled.

I first wrote about the issue of sexuality in my June 2001 newsletter *Straight Talk* in a tribute to movie actress Vivien Leigh. I had recently watched a documentary on this talented actress from *Gone With the Wind* fame and heard the word *"nymphomaniac"* used to describe her. It wasn't the first time I heard that description attributed to Leigh. Each time Leigh was linked to this description, I became enraged. I know how it feels to be accused of this derogatory word because it happened to me in my own marriage. Thousands of women have told me that their gay husbands have accused them, too, of this awful word. What made me so angry is that this poor soul was married to Sir Lawrence Olivier, a known gay/bisexual man. His exploits with actor Danny Kaye (no relation to me) were well known in Hollywood circles. It is so much easier for gay husbands to degrade us by making us feel inadequate as women than to tell us the truth of why they think that our *normal* sexual drives are excessive.

In a number of my monthly *Straight Talk* newsletters, I wrote about sexuality and the shame and embarrassment that we feel within ourselves after years of having our internal feelings of sexual worth torn down layer by layer. I know how I felt when I was married to my gay husband when it came to sexuality. I remember how I quietly cried from humiliation when

35

he accused me of being a nymphomaniac just because I had normal sexual wants and desires. I wasn't asking for too much—*the problem was that I was asking at all*. A gay man in almost every case feels that it is an imposition for him to have sex with a straight woman. He'll do it, but he'll let you knew that it's no pleasure. Maybe he won't say it verbally, but he will say it through his body language.

In order to understand sexuality better in general, allow me to digress for a few moments and give some historical perspectives. I met my gay husband in the late 1970's. It was during the time when the sexual revolution was in full gear. Best selling books had been written a decade earlier as part of the women's movement in this country. In the years when I was growing up, sexuality was not something that was spoken about except among close friends in small circles. Going to your parents for advice was just something we didn't do because it was still a taboo subject. Our mothers and grandmothers were raised in a generation where sexuality was part of the package of being a wife. It was not a function that was to be enjoyed, just part of the wifely obligation that came as payment for having a man go to work and support you. Those things started to change while I was growing up.

I was a child of the 1960's when the sexual revolution was in full force. Sex was definitely the "in thing" by the time I reached my late teens. In 1968, at the age of 17, I moved to California from my hometown of Philadelphia to live with my father who had relocated there after his divorce from my mother. This was a period of time and a place where there were no limits—on anything. The drug revolution was in full swing. Everything and anything was acceptable when it came to sex.

As teenagers, we took advantage of our raging hormones and just did it to make ourselves feel good. Back then there was no AIDS. The worst that could happen was a sexually transmitted disease that was easily treated with a week's worth of penicillin. I remember going to those free clinics that were jammed packed with people waiting for an impersonal and often

36

painful gynecological examination to determine if it was syphilis or gonorrhea. We all breathed in a sigh of relief when it was gonorrhea. There was actually no shame or embarrassment when a sexual partner called you to inform you that there was a "problem." You just picked yourself up, went to the clinic, and took care of it. We were the "love children" generation because we were sexually liberated. No hang-ups, no inhibitions. Sex just became a recreational activity.

By the time I moved back to Philadelphia in 1970, the East Coast was in tune with the times. It was not unusual for people to have very casual one-night sexual encounters with no emotional attachments. Now everyone knew that **sex** was no longer a forbidden word, and people were talking about how wonderful it was. Women were no longer just recipients of men's natural functions. We wanted to be fulfilled and satisfied. We wanted our needs be acknowledged. No longer would women stand for men just jumping on top of them and getting their kicks. Now there was going to be an exchange of mutual pleasure.

It took a lot of men time to catch on to this. They had been spoiled for centuries by thinking that they could just do it when they wanted and how they wanted. And it wasn't their fault entirely either. They didn't have teachers to tell them that it was their job to make a woman feel as good as they were feeling. They now first had to learn.

This must have been a difficult time for gay men who were passing through life in marriages with straight women because the word was out. One of the great benefits of the sexual revolution was that it gave women a forum to learn about sexual behavior. That's not to say that all women were participants, but they at least were hearing the talk. They learned that there were expected "norms" when it came to sex, and they weren't having them. It made a lot of these women start to wonder what was wrong in their marriages.

By the time I met my gay husband in the late 1970's, I was fully sexually experienced. I had numerous meaningless sexual encounters over the years, but I also had a previous marriage and long-term live-in relationship. Maybe I didn't know everything about sex, but I knew enough to understand how great it could be with the right partner. Within several weeks of meeting my future husband, we found ourselves in bed together. I remember that in spite of Michael's efforts, I was not satisfied at the end of it. And several days later when we did it again, I was feeling the same sense of frustration.

This was a dilemma for me. I was crazy about this man and knew instinctively that he was going to be my husband in the future. While he seemed to feel satisfied with our lovemaking, I wasn't. I also knew that if I was planning to spend a lifetime with him, I would never be happy if I had to spend it feeling unsatisfied in bed. While some women don't seem to have a problem communicating this thought to their lovers, I, like many, did. It was just so difficult to tell someone this kind of information because it is so personal. I was worried that he would take it as an insult. What man wants to be told that he is not a great lover? What man's ego is strong enough to not take this information personally and feel rejected? And yet, I was selfish enough for myself to know that I could never last in a relationship without feeling satisfied sexually—at least sometimes.

I was braver in those earlier days of the relationship than I was in the days that followed. I found the courage to tell Michael that there were things I needed sexually that were just missing. I told him in a very sensitive way—so I thought. Unfortunately, Michael didn't take it well. He was very defensive. First response: *"I've never had any woman complain before."* My translation: **It must be my fault**. Next response: *"I feel satisfied. I can't understand why you're not."* My translation: **Maybe I'm just too sexually demanding**. I retreated momentarily to think about how to proceed.

After our next encounter several days later, he asked me if I felt any better. Nothing had really changed so I didn't exactly know why he expected a different response. But I braved it again using a different strategy. I told him that every woman was different. Some women may feel satisfied just from penetration, but I needed other stimulation to have an orgasm. Response*: "That's ridiculous. I've never been with a woman before who needed that to feel satisfied."* Of course, I was under the false illusion that he had been with many women before based on what he kept telling me, However, I was not ready to give up yet. I told him that obviously my body worked differently than other women's, and he shouldn't take it personally. **It was me—not him**. I told him in a short, concise manner what my body needed. It was so difficult to express this because I was never good at talking about sex. And so the next time, I guided his fingers to where I wanted them, and he "accommodated" my needs. And oh, how I praised him for making me happy—or shall I say happier.

I say happier because you can just tell when someone is doing something because they are accommodating you, not because they enjoy doing it. And that's exactly how I felt. I also hoped in time he wouldn't think that it was any big deal, because it wasn't as far as I was concerned. What came so naturally to other men seemed to be like such a chore for him. I remember arming myself with four or five books one night and bringing them home to show him that this is what women need to feel satisfied. I carefully put bookmarkers in the sections where clitoral stimulation was mentioned as the way to a woman's orgasm. After showing him the first one, he told me to stop—he got the drift. He accepted that he would have to do something that was obviously "not his thing" to make me happy, and I felt as if I had won the battle even if I didn't seem to win the war. This was actually a shallow victory in retrospect. No woman wants to feel as if her husband is doing her a favor when he is making love to her, and that's always how I felt.

We had a whirlwind courtship that was fast and intense. We married three months after we met. There was no hesitancy on his part as far as marriage. Having a family was a dream that he always had. It wasn't hard to keep up the pretense of a sexual relationship for a short amount of time. In fact, on our honeymoon, I remember how determined Michael was to have sex with me everyday because he always wanted me to "remember our honeymoon." And I went along with it because I thought it was making him happy. It wasn't spontaneous—it was a planned activity. And although I can't say that it was memorable, I can say that I do remember it because it was so calculated.

In the early months of our marriage, our sex life started to deteriorate. We went from having sex twice a week to once a week. By the third or fourth month it was every other week. Then it was reduced to every few weeks. But the problem wasn't the frequency as much as it was the humiliation that went along with it.

After the early months of the marriage when sex started fading, I mentioned it to Michael. This was after trying not to mention it while trying instead to make it happen but failing. At first, the excuses seemed valid. A headache, a virus, a hard week at work, financial pressures, late nights with friends, family visits, overwhelming exhaustion, etc. etc. etc. Of course, once of month there was the excuse of my menstrual cycle so that was always a better week for my husband. No need to come up with excuses that week because it seemed that's when his libido was in full swing. Of course, my menstrual cramps didn't quite put me in the mood for romance. And, if we were to have sex during that week, it was a one-way street driving up his side of the road. It took me a few months to get smart to that monthly ritual of, "Honey, let's make love now." How convenient.

When I finally had to verbalize my concern about the problem, Michael's first response was that it was natural for a couple's sex life to fall off. I replied that after years of marriage that might be true, but not after months. And we were young. We were only in our late 20's. Feeling duly pressured, he'd do it. It seemed as though we were having increased arguments as the night progressed and often over nothing. This made it convenient not to think about making love as a way to end the evening. I went to bed crying silently a lot. And sometimes it

40

wasn't silent. But it didn't seem to matter. He slept through it no matter if it was loud or soft.

In my greatest moments of frustration while we argued, I threw sex into the battleground. That's when the insults were furled in my face. I was *too* demanding. I was *too* pushy, *too* aggressive. My sexual needs were "abnormal." And then the word that stabbed me the hardest was blurted out. **Nympho-maniac.** No woman likes to hear that word when it is an accusation. It hastened my retreat and I quickly backed off from discussing it further. Mission accomplished.

This is one of the worst parts of being the wife of a gay man. You are slowly—or in some cases quickly—robbed of your natural instincts as a woman. You start to believe that you are an inadequate lover. After all, if you were a good lover, your husband would want you, right? You can imagine how confusing this must be to women who are not sexually experienced. The majority of women I've worked with were not sexually experienced when they married their gay husbands. In my first book, when I wrote about the prototype of a woman that a gay man seeks out for marriage consciously or unconsciously, one of the characteristics on the top of my list is a woman with limited sexual experience. After all, what you don't know can't hurt you. If a woman has never had sexual experience before, it's easy to be "tricked" into thinking what is good sex and what is normal frequency of sex.

Although it's hard to believe, even in this day and age many women are still not sexually experienced and don't understand about sex. It is due to a variety of factors. Religious beliefs play a big part in this. And so does a new sense of morality that was brought about in the face of AIDS that swept through the country in the 1980's and 1990's. When people learned that sex could be a death sentenced, they were more comfortable saying *"no thanks"* than *"yes."* The practice of multiple sex partners lost its popularity. The message was loud and clear—the safest sex was **no sex.**

Women waited longer than they did in the past before entering into sexual relationships. Numerous women write me that they spent more time getting to know their men before jumping into bed with them. Many held out for marriage to make sure that they would avoid dealing with this disease, and then demanded proof from their mates through blood tests. Other sexually transmitted diseases started to develop at the same time. None of them had the fatal consequences of AIDS, but they were still horrible. Herpes became a rampant sexually transmitted disease that could not be resolved by a dose of antibiotics. Once you had it, you were stuck with it for life. And so the previous years of sexual revolution came to a dead halt, and women waited or limited their sexual activity.

AIDS also created a wave of mass hysteria when it was first discovered. All fingers pointed to homosexuals, and homo-phobia was greatly heightened in this country. So little was known about this deadly disease at first other than it was killing gay men by the thousands. In the early years, it was nicknamed "The Gay Disease." Straight people felt a false sense of security because you didn't hear about straight people dying from it. Then when straight people started dying, it was because they were infected with gay blood during a transfusion in surgery or when transfused for hemophilia. And when straight men who didn't need blood transfusions started dying, it was because they were with prostitutes who gave it to them. These prostitutes were drug addicts and contracted this disease through shared needles. And then IV drug users who weren't prostitutes were coming down with AIDS. As long as society's "undesirables" were the ones getting infected, people didn't seem too concerned about themselves. I remember so many comments made by ignorant religious people claiming that this was God's punishment for gay people and using AIDS as proof that homosexuality was sinful.

AIDS paranoia was everywhere. I remember when movie star Rock Hudson died from AIDS, everyone was so worried about his female co-star Linda Evans because he kissed her durIng a television series. They feared that she was put at risk from the kiss and could be infected from that love scene. People thought that AIDS was airborne and warned you not to get too close to gay people. Drinking from the same cup was enough to send someone into a panic. It was so frightening. In my book **"The Gay Husband Checklist for Women Who Wonder,"** I related the story about my son's nursery school horror experience when the parents of the children petitioned the school to have him thrown out. They found out his father was gay when one of the mothers saw me on the Sally Jesse Raphael show, and when my son went to the hospital for some minor surgery, they assumed he had AIDS and didn't want their kids in school with him. This was in 1986, and it was very devastating to me. The school stood by my son, but the pain of others' ignorance stayed with me for a long time.

Keeping that hysteria in mind, you can only imagine how many homosexual men who may have been "out of the closet" so to speak started running a top speed to get back in. I was jumping into that closet with them because of how my son was treated even though it was a mis-perception based on someone's hysteria. That's when I ended all public television appearances.

The fear of discrimination and persecution made gay men try harder than ever to pass into the straight world. And I can say with confidence that for those men who could pull off a straight sexual performance, no matter how infrequently or how unpleasant the prospect seemed, marriage became a viable answer to the outside hysteria and the internal fear. I have spoken to many a gay husband who confirmed that for me through the years. If there was any chance to "change," this was the time to take the chance.

With women reversing their sexual revolution days and gay men trying harder than ever to be straight, it is easy to see why there were such increasing numbers of gay men seeking the security of a wife, family, and home. And it is also easy to see why women more readily accepted explanations of *"let's wait until we're married before having sex"* as an acceptable explanation. Some of these men I've spoken to said they were willing to live with their gay fantasies inside the confines of their marriages to their heterosexual wives. Others were hoping that those gay feelings would magically disappear if they loved their wives enough. And still others thought that they could pull off being straight indefinitely. And that's why I conclude that the overwhelming majority of women who write to me for help are somewhere between 45 and 55 years old and have been married between 10 and 20 years.

These husbands tried to be straight. Really they did. In my heart, I believe that almost all gay men who marry want it to work. There's no ill intention. They are hoping against hope that somehow, things will work themselves out. Many of these men suppressed their feelings for years. They just put those thoughts in the very back compartment of their minds hoping that if they pushed them back far enough, they would disappear once and for all. Some pushed hard enough to allow themselves not even to think the unthinkable. A few—not many—even carried off sexual relations with their wives on a regular basis and believed that the "straight thing" had kicked in for real. None of these men have been able to articulate exactly what it was that made that pushed back, sealed tight box start to move forward and untie itself. Maybe it's because society eased-up on homophobia. Maybe it's because the mind can only be in denial for so long. For many, it was the lack of feeling of fulfillment. No matter how good their marriages were, and no matter how loving their wives were, there was something missing—namely a man.

I like working with women who have horrible and destructive marriages. The answers are so much easier and clear cut. But for those wives who have been in good marriages, it's another story. These are the women who suffer the most. They just can't grasp it. How does a man who was so dedicated to his family for 10, 15, 20, 30, and even 40 years change so much in (usually) such a short time? I always ask these women in retrospect if there were any signs, any hints, any clues. Rarely do they say yes. They were totally blindsided. Several have even told me that they had an on-going sex life throughout the marriage with no break in the action. Well, at least two out of every thousand or so.

Let me just emphasize again, the marriages that are happy prior to the gay men coming out are not the majority of those that exist. Most marriages are problematic from the early stages. These men feel "trapped" and often blame their wives for their unhappiness. It's evident when it comes time to making love. That's when they really let you know just how "trapped" they feel.

Having sex with a gay man leaves you feeling empty. Even if your husband tells you how much he loves you, there is something very mechanical and calculated about his moves. In most cases, it lacks the passion and fun that sex with a straight man offers. And perhaps that's why I keep referring to it as "sex" rather than "making love." The reason for that is when a straight man makes love to you, he is thinking about you and acting like he's happy to be with you. With a gay man, he is distracted. He's there in body, but not in spirit. It is not unusual for him to fantasize about being with a man in order for him to maintain an erection or to have an orgasm.

It kind of reminds me of a reversal of roles. Prior to the sexual revolution which started women "demanding" that they be an equal partner in the act of love making, many of them went through the motions of having sex to please their husbands. They didn't find it particularly enjoyable or fulfilling. They did it because they had to do it because it was their "wifely obligation." When a gay man makes love to his wife, he too does it because he has to do it. It's expected of him to do it whether he wants to or not. The main difference is that women had to do it for years until the sexual urges of their husbands declined, while gay men stop doing after a few years because they can't pretend anymore. Men, by nature, are far more sexual than women. They don't have to personalize sex to feel fulfilled—it is more of a "bodily" function. Women, on the other hand, do personalize sex. When a man seems annoyed or disinterested, she takes it very personally. And this is where the roads part.

When a woman feels as if her husband would rather be anywhere but in bed with her, she starts to wonder what *she* is doing wrong. If she knew that her husband was gay, that would certainly explain it. But when she doesn't know, it doesn't explain it. And these women personalize the failure of their sex life as *their failure*. Why doesn't my husband want me….why doesn't he find me arousing…..what am I doing wrong…..maybe if I was more attractive…..etc., etc., etc. What they haven't figured out is there is nothing they can do to make their husbands find them more attractive—namely because they are women and their husbands desire men.

I hear horror stories. I worked with a professional model who was perfect to her photographers and public, but not to her husband. To make herself more attractive to him, she surgically had breast implants added to her body. She was distressed because he did not respond to her any differently. When she found out several months later that he was gay, she finally understood why it didn't make a difference. I've heard quite a number of the breast implant, gastric bypass, and liposuction stories in women's quests for making them more desirable to their husbands. And each time I hear it, I become overwhelmed with anger. I explain that the only thing that might make a difference is a penis implant. Thank goodness no one so far has opted for that alternative!

They say that sex is the part of any couple's relationship that takes the least amount of time. Maybe the part about the amount of time is true. But it is such an important part of a relationship because it creates intimacy, closeness, and trust. A healthy sexual relationship builds a sense of sexual and self-esteem in a woman because she feels desirable. I had the good fortune in my life to learn this.

In 1994, I began a new adventure with my soulmate. It's been a wonderful, fulfilling experience for me emotionally and sexually. I learned how different the love of a straight man is from the love of a gay man. I also learned how long a fulfilling sexual relationship can sustain itself over a long extended period of time when you find the right partner.

Making love is an important part of our relationship. It keeps it filled with passion and excitement. It's a beautiful way for us to express our love for each other. Instead of sex dwindling and disappearing early in the game as it often does with a gay husband, our sex life has maintained a high level of frequency all these years later. It gives us an added treasure to look forward to and each week. In between, it brings us closer with holding, touching, and caressing as a sort of aftermath. This keeps our love alive and flourishing.

It also builds an important part of the relationship as a whole—namely "Intimacy." This establishes feelings that will fill the void in future years when circumstances may limit our sexual activity. During those times, we can still lay in each others arms, hold each other, gently kiss each other, and know that what we had before we will soon have again. Over the eighteen years that we have been together, there have been short periods of life's circumstances that have created down times in the bedroom such as illness and external family problems. But we always know that when the problem is over, our lovemaking will resume. And because we have this as our foundation in our relationship, the intimacy holds us over through those rough spots. We are now of "senior status," and yet to see us, you would think we are young lovers.

I feel very sorry for women with gay husbands who have never experienced other sex. It upsets me when I receive letters from women saying that *not* having sex with their gay husband is *not* a big deal. When I question these women about previous sexual experiences with straight men, in most cases, they never had any. They have learned to suppress their natural sexual desires in the same way that their husbands have suppressed theirs for men when getting married. The difference is that in time, men can't keep it suppressed anymore. They act on their needs while their wives just continue to be sexual hermits.

Out of the thousands of letters I receive each year, one of my saddest was from an educated, lovely woman who has been married for 30 years. For 30 years there was no sexual activity in her marriage. Her husband claimed he was sexually dysfunctional after the "I do's," and she loved him enough to believe it. She accepted he had an "illness" and decided she would learn to live without sex.   After 30 years, she found him on the Internet looking at gay pornography. He meekly admitted that this is what turns him on. Thirty years is a lifetime to live in a marriage with no sex. She accepted his excuse for all those years and <u>didn't want him to feel inadequate</u>, so she bit the bullet so to say and allowed her sex life to die before it ever got started. This woman had been robbed of what was rightfully hers to have-- namely a life with passion and intimacy.

This is one of the sadder stories. But there are many worse scenarios. At least this husband took the blame for being sexually dysfunctional after 30 years. It's so much worse when a husband is gay but blames his wife for <u>their failure in their sex life</u>. Often the harsh words of, *"If only you were thinner, if only you were more supportive, if only your were less demanding"* throws the problem in our laps when we are not the problem at all.   But most women aren't sexually savvy enough to understand this.

I was very sexually experienced when I married my gay husband, and yet, I bought into these accusations making me believe that our sexual problems were due to me. I knew it wasn't me when the marriage began, but in time, the self-doubt started kicking in. Within a few short years, I felt totally inadequate as a woman. This sense of personal rejection hurt so much. Worse yet, it impacted on my ability to have the confidence to begin a new relationship with a man for many years after the marriage ended. I can only imagine how much worse it is for women who are not sexually experienced and have nothing else to compare it to. It is so easy to blame yourself because you just don't know. The gay husbands of these women are well aware of that lack of sexual experience and count on the fact that they won't think that it's them—it's you.

People who hear these stories--but who haven't lived them--ask how stupid can we be. The truth is that it doesn't happen immediately. It's a process that happens over time. In the beginning, almost all of the gay men do have sexual relations with their wives. They may not be great, or very often, but they do happen. This is what confuses us. Our husbands are able to perform, have an erection, and in many cases, able to have an orgasm. At least for a while, that is. Some of them even find it pleasurable because after all, it is a sexual release. Therefore, these gay men can derive sexual satisfaction from a straight woman—but it is never going to be satisfying enough to keep away those nagging attractions and overwhelming desires for men. Some will give it their best tries, but ultimately, they feel they are missing something that you can't give them no matter what you do to try to fix it. There are no fixes here. Their natural inborn need for men will eventually surface. Sometimes it's in a year—sometimes it's in 10 or 20 years. But the threat is always there, looming overhead.

Numerous straight women also box themselves into accepting the decline of sexual intimacy in their marriages. They buy into their husbands' excuses or abuses and let the sexuality part of them go into hibernation or wither and die all together. It is not unusual for a wife to blame herself for her husband's homosexual thoughts or desires. Some gay husbands are cruel enough to blame their wives, stating that they weren't this way before the marriage. Imagine how disheartening it feels when you think that you are so inadequate as a woman that your husband has to turn to men. This is when women start playing the dangerous game that I call the *"If Only"* game.

It goes like this. **"If only I could be a better wife….*if only I was more attractive…if only I was better as a lover…if only I***

49

was a better housekeeper, if only I wasn't so demanding...if only I could lose more weight....if only I was smarter...if only, if only, if only...then maybe he could love me enough not to think of men.

And while we are playing the **"If Only"** game, some husbands are playing the other mind-twister game, which I call the **"Blame Game."** This is where gay husbands come closest to revealing the truth by throwing in your face, **"If I became gay, who could blame me? After all, you are too demanding... always making too many sexual demands...always complaining about something...gaining weight...acting jealous...being possessive ...too sloppy....too suspicious... all consuming...**and the list goes on. I mention these games because they hit directly into the sexuality issues.

It is very difficult if you blame yourself for the sexual failures in your marriage to start repairing the damage to your sexual esteem. You feel unworthy of being a sexual being with normal needs and wants. You also doubt your ability to please a man because the man you have been living with makes it clear that you are not a sex-pleaser. Getting back into the swing of life after marriage or a relationship with a gay man can be very difficult.

Straight wives handle the sexuality problems in various ways after the marriages are over. Some jump right into sexual relationships to prove to themselves that they are "normal," at least in bed. They are trying to counteract the damage that has progressed over the years from living with their gay husbands. Other women are petrified to start a relationship with a man for long periods of time. I was one of those women. It took me eleven years to allow those wounds to heal, and even at that, I still had some scars that lasted for more years to come.

The good news is that there is hope for every woman whose sexual esteem has been broken and battered like mine was. I felt so deflated as a woman and as a sex partner. I was content living in a state of celibacy and suppressing that side of my human need. Then one day, my longing to be with a man awakened, and I knew I was ready to love and make love again.

I was out there meeting men for nearly two years before my soulmate came sailing into my life. During that period, I met dozens of men. I had some short-term relationships and even a few shorter encounters. I was ready to awaken the side of me that had died during my marriage. I was awkward at first because it had been so long. But when the right moment came, I took advantage of it. I know I wasn't at my best at first because I was so nervous, but I certainly enjoyed the passion of a straight man. It felt so nice to have someone want to fulfill that need and do it happily instead of feeling like I was forcing him. It wasn't perfect the first time or even the tenth time, but it kept getting better as I started gaining back my sexual confidence.

Yes, it's scary starting this side of life over again, but it is so worth it. All women are born with sexuality. Women who are married to gay men have had that side suppressed or deadened by their spouse. We just learn to give up on that part of us and to bury it thinking that this is the natural course of marriage or a relationship. Please know that it can be revived and brought back to life.

I finally learned, for lack of a better term, about **"REAL SEX."** This is different than having sex with a gay man. Gay husband egos aside, sex with a gay man is at best, satisfactory sex, or perhaps functionary sex. But real true passion—well, it's just not.

Now I know the difference. Not only did I have a gay husband, I also had a couple of gay boyfriends in my younger years. We did it, but it always left something to be desired. My ex-husband wasn't a failure on those occasions when we had sex. But it always seemed like he had to try so hard—almost forced—after the honeymoon was over. And there's nothing to deflate your ego more than thinking that a man is doing you a favor by making love to you—especially a man who loves you.

I recently asked my gay husband if he could think back to the days when we were sexually involved prior to and shortly

51

after the marriage. I told him that I needed his honest, objective opinion about our sex life together. Did he really enjoy it? Did he look forward to it? Was it a hardship for him? He told me that in the beginning, he actually did enjoy it. Having sex with me was working toward his goal of getting married and having a family. He was hoping that I would be the solution to his fantasy of the American dream. He still did not consider himself gay at that point although he had already had numerous gay sexual encounters. But he felt that he was straight because he never had an emotional entanglement with these guys. There was no kissing, hugging or intimacy with the guys—it was just sex.

I hear that from many gay men who cross over to the straight side for a while. They are not trying to fool us—they are trying to fool Mother Nature. Or they are hoping that Mother Nature has been playing a joke on them because they are able to perform with a woman to some degree. My ex-husband was certainly adequate enough as a lover to fool me. It was never a great sex life, but it was a good sex life for the first few months after we got past the initial problems of what it takes to satisfy me. There was nothing that out of whack that would make me suspect that he was gay.

All these years later, I am happy to say that I have learned about the beauty of sexuality. I attribute that to my renewed sexual excitement with my soulmate. As I mentioned earlier, after eighteen years, our sexual relationship is still top of the line. My soulmate is playful and passionate. He aims to please because he gets satisfaction out of pleasing me—and it turns him on instead of off. Every encounter is an adventure. We don't have sex—we make love. This is perhaps the real difference. Making love to someone is an important way of expressing love. Wanting to please your partner before pleasing yourself is the most unselfish form of showing love. Making sure that your partner is satisfied shows the real nature of giving love. I have come to enjoy new aspects of lovemaking that I never dreamt existed. <u>And I don't have to scheme about how I can have him make love to me</u>. He is always ready, able, and willing to go. Even after all of these years, our sex life is continually peaking. This man makes me feel as if I am the most desirable woman in the world.

He hasn't noticed yet the seventy pounds I've gained in the past few years because his love for me blinds him to my imperfections. I haven't noticed that he's not Steven Segal yet because in my eyes, that's whom he looks like. Maybe our lives are like the movie "The Enchanted Cottage," where two people appear physically to each other only to be what they see in each other, even if no one else can see it. But isn't that what true love really is?

My soulmate has never calls me a ***"nymphomaniac"*** That's because I'm not. I never was. I am just a normal woman with very normal sexual needs. He has cultivated my sexuality and taught me that I can reach new heights of enjoyment. It is easy to keep me sexually interested because my partner never allows our sex life to become boring or mundane. He is a straight man—a straight man who appreciates a straight woman.

Let this be a lesson for all of you. Never give up the part of you that helps maintain your identity as a woman. Give yourself a chance to be loved again. Look for your soulmate because chances are, he is out there looking for you. Don't be afraid to take the journey even if you never find him. You will find some wonderful straight men out there that can make you feel like the wonderful woman you are and satisfy your natural born needs that are a treasure in life.

Gay Husbands
Come in Different Varieties

You might think that the term "gay husband" would be as simple as that. You have a husband. He comes to terms with himself at some point during the marriage. He discloses this information to you. You both deal with the pain and then make decisions that will affect your future. That's the ideal way that this "un-ideal" situation should work at best.

Unfortunately, that's not the way it works for many women. I venture to say from my experience, that at least half of the women I have counseled have situations that are far more complicated than even the complexities of the "ideal" situation.

There are married gay men who won't leave the marriage or for that matter, won't leave the closet. This is a subject that can never be talked about enough because it seems to be a stumbling block for so many straight wives who can't get their husbands to "come clean" with the truth about their homosexuality. I get dozens of letters monthly from women who confront their husbands with concrete evidence in hand but still get angry denials with distorted truths. The explanations/ excuses range from, *"Those gay pornographic magazines belong to a co-worker and I'm just hiding them here for him,"* to *"I have no clue how those websites got on our computer."*

For those women whose husbands eventually tell you the truth, count yourselves as lucky even though you may not feel that way at the time of the shocking news. No doubt hearing the word **gay** is devastating, but **not** hearing it is even worse.

Women frequently write to me for advice because their husbands or ex-husbands will not admit their homosexuality. These women know the truth. They have stumbled on it one way or another. It has smacked them in the face through hidden websites, email, pornography, letters, hotel receipts, phone bills, etc. And yet, their husbands just keep lying or denying. They are not ready to be honest--and may never be ready. Some men will never be able to accept their homosexuality because it is too painful or embarrassing to deal with.

These men in hiding can also be broken into various classifications because they too are not all the same in their behaviors and attitudes. Some people refer to these men as "Bisexual," but I have been able to break down the classifications much further. I have divided these men into subcategories that more accurately describe them.

In my previous book, I wrote a chapter about **Bisexuality.** Basically, I negated the term bisexual by showing that it was a more palatable way for gay men and their straight wives to live within the confines of marriage—or shall I say exist. It sounds much trendier to say "bisexual" rather than gay, but this also gives the wife a false sense of hope. Straight wives think that if a husband can make a choice about his sexual preference, then with enough love and nurturing, he will choose the straight way—meaning her. I am always saddened when people waste years of their lives living on false hope.

What the term **"bisexual"** does for women who are determined to stay in their marriages is allow them to differentiate (or rather justify) love from sex. Their **"bisexual"** husbands claim that their wives meet their "real" love and emotional needs. It's just their libido that needs to be satisfied by a man. It's nothing personal. Or, to rephrase a popular song, *"What's sex got to do, got to do with it? What's sex, it's not love or emotion."* And some wives live like that forever. As long as their husbands come home to them and their families, and as long as their sexual relationships are nothing more than libido encounters, it's do-able. As long as the "**bisexual**" husband has sex strictly with a **"Libido Man," (a gay man who has come to terms with himself and who is just looking for sexual pleasure)** and if that man is only an abstract thought in the wife's mind versus a visual effect, she can do it. She can live with it. These are the women who tell me, "Well, in heterosexual marriages, the sex fades in time anyway." Gay married men claiming to be "bi" tell me the same story. They must be reading the same literature.

Then there are the men whom I have named the **"Limbo Men."** Their whole lives are lived in a state of limbo. They are **emotionally** straight, but **sexually** gay. They are "caught" or "stuck" in between two worlds, never feeling totally comfortable in either world. But they are much more comfortable *"passing"* in the straight world where they are accepted as part of mainstream society by their friends, co-workers, and family members—except for you, of course.

All married gay men go through "**limbo**" for a period of time. In other words, they are stuck in between both worlds hoping that by wanting the straight world badly enough they will be able to "cross over" into it. They keep thinking that if they play the role long enough, they will become transformed into the part, not just play the part as an actor. Limbo Men are different from other gay men who eventually come to terms with themselves. The Limbo Men will stay in their marriages, and on some level, acknowledge that they are gay, even if it is only to themselves. They will usually allude to their wives that they have a problem or leave little clues behind, kind of hoping that you'll bring it up. And if you confront them, they won't get up in your face and start screaming at you that you're "crazy." They may come up with stories like, "I've had gay fantasies, but I'm not gay," or "I've had one or two sexual encounters with males in my youth, but I realized that I am straight." Whew. Take a big sigh of relief.

Then there is another kind of gay men who are the most difficult kind to live with. I call these men the *"Straight Gay Men"* because they are gay men living in straight men's clothing. No matter what happens, they will never admit to being gay, not even to themselves. They are in total denial and have all intentions of remaining there forever and ever.

The real ***Straight Gay Men*** have no sense of remorse for what they are doing to their wives. In fact, they often feel as if they are the victims in their marriage and strike back at their spouses in an emotionally or physically abusive manner. They blame the wives for their unhappiness and never have a clue about the emotional damage they are doing to these women whom they promised to love, cherish, and respect. They constantly criticize and demoralize their wives, when in fact there is nothing that their wives could possibly do to make them feel happy or fulfilled. Their wives are women, and they are gay men.

These are the men who will never leave their marriages. They are not going to meet some nice gay man who will bring them happiness. That would be unthinkable. They will stay married until the day they die, leading a painful existence and transferring that pain unto their wives. More accurately, pouring that pain upon their wives like pouring salt onto a wound. We all know that misery loves company, and these men are happy to make you as miserable as they are.

These men are usually very homophobic—and they mean it for real. The thought of "gay men" is sickening to them. They view them as perverted and distorted. They will taunt and ridicule them, This is how they mentally respond to their own form of self-hatred. To accept gays would mean they would be accepting that part of them that they work so hard to hide and reject. They are also ultra paranoid that someone might "misinterpret" any compassion they may have towards homosexuality, even if they had any. This might point the finger of suspicion their way.

And guess what the irony of the **Straight Gay Man** is? If a woman finally gets smart enough to walk away from the marriage, in almost all cases, he will go and find another woman for a relationship. This is the most frightening aspect of all. Some other unsuspecting woman is going to get trapped, or rather zapped. I see this too often. When women write to me about how hurt they are because their gay ex-husbands are dating other women, their hurt seems even greater than the women whose husbands come out and find men. They really personalize it even though they know the truth. It's not like they want their gay husbands back, but it's like an extra slap in the face to the women on an emotional level. Just thinking that there are other women out there that can fulfill the needs of their ex-gay husbands is very painful.

If it's any consolation, rest assured that whatever woman is unfortunate enough to hook up with your gay husband will be just as unhappy as you were. After the dust settles and the new woman is reliving your hell, she'll be wondering what's wrong with her. The worst part about this is that the new woman will always be told how much better of a wife you were than she is. That's how your ex-husband will be able to start stripping her self and sexual esteem down. And she won't catch on to the gay thing for a lot longer than it took you. After all, he married before--he married again. How can he be gay? Most likely, he had children with you. This must mean that he's not gay, right? Some unsuspecting women will inevitably be forced to deal with your nightmare. Tragic, isn't it?

So often, these **"Straight Gay Men"** and **"Limbo Men"** husbands luck out. They have wives who are much kinder and more understanding than the average woman. In my book *"The Gay Husband Checklist for Women Who Wonder,"* I have a chapter about the prototype of woman that gay men who marry seek out. It's not an accident that wives of gay men are better than the average wife. These are the women who will keep trying every little trick in the book thinking someday they will get their husbands hooked. The women live an accepted existence, accepting the crumbs in the marriage while trying to turn those crumbs into a cake. Sadly, they rarely are able to gather enough crumbs to make a cookie, forget a cake. It is truly a tragedy and waste of human life.

Understanding the Gay Husband Metamorphosis, or "It's All About Them!"

It's interesting to see how many of our ex-husbands like to keep us involved in their personal relationships after the marriage has ended. They have this need to share with us the details of their new love lives and come to us for solace when their relationships aren't working out. I don't see that happening very often in straight relationships. I think part of it is because many of us continue to have feelings on some level for our gay husbands. As ultimate caretakers, which most of us are, we still don't want to see them get hurt even when we are hurting from them. It is not unusual for straight wives to get "sucked in" to listening to the problems that their husbands now face when they enter the gay lifestyle.

I am someone who is guilty of this. Whenever my ex calls me with sad stories or glad stories about his romantic relationships, I listen. Sometimes I was angry with myself for being dragged into these dramas. Part of me wanted to say, "leave me alone," but the other part of me felt the need to listen because my ex wanted to share with me. I see this happening so often with other women who were married to gay men. I can't imagine straight men behaving this way, or I can't imagine women willing to listen to the love exploits of their straight ex-husbands.

The difference is that many of us still have feelings of love for our gay husbands. Our marriages ended because of circumstances—not, in most cases, because we didn't love our husbands anymore. And even though we go through all the stages of mourning the death of our marriage, including denial, anger, even bitterness and hatred, in many cases, after we pass through these stages, we come to terms and acceptance with the situation, and we are able to move on.

The part of us that loved our husbands is still there. For many of us, these men will be part of our futures because we are tied together through our children. That loving, caring side of us is who we are. When our exes come to us crying the blues, we end up being the cheer-up team. I know it's hard to believe this if you're presently going through the trauma, but I can attest to this from many women who later befriend their ex-husbands. And as time starts healing your initial wounds, and your life starts moving ahead, it is not uncommon to reach a mental state of *acceptance*, which is not the same as *approval*. It means that you can accept your husband is gay, it's not your fault, and life is moving on to new grounds for you.

I also hear many gay men complain that their wives seem bitter and unwilling to move on to "acceptance." But one of the things that slow the growth of reaching this stage of acceptance for women is the ex-husband's lack of accountability to the family after he comes out and decides to lead a gay lifestyle. Too often, I see men who were previous candidates for "Father of the Year" become practically invisible to the children they were so devoted to for years in the past. There is such an astonishing turn around, that the wives cannot believe or understand it.

This behavior creates a delay in the recovery process for women because now they are more confused than ever. It's one thing when the shock of the sexuality is going through your mind, but then the sudden personality turn around only adds to the pain. It is incomprehensible to women that the husbands who lovingly took the kids to the movies, museums, restaurants, sang them to sleep, kissed their bruises, rushed to their teacher conferences, coached their Little Leagues, etc. are now in a space that seems to have nothing but distant memories. They are exploring their new world with limited time to think about those special moments that we still long for and continue to reminisce over.

It never ceases to amaze me how dependable, responsible men suddenly become insensitive to our new roles as single mothers forced to make a multitude of adjustments and changes in our lives within a very short time span. Remember, when a man decides to come out to his wife, he has had a long time to think about it. He is on his way out of the marriage long before the news is revealed—at least mentally. He is thinking, planning, fantasizing, and, in many cases, acting on his new found sexuality. The wife, on the other hand, is living in a vacuum. She has no idea that her husband is someone whom she has no clue about. She is living in a secure womb of marriage that may not be fulfilling, but a marriage nonetheless.

The majority of times, straight wives love their gay husbands even "harder" than women with straight husbands. Since we feel a sense of sexual rejection early in the marriage and internalize that it is our fault, we try so much more to please our husbands and be good wives. We think that even though we can't keep them happy in the bedroom, we'll at least keep them happy in the marriage. In many cases, we are deluded into thinking we have a successful marriage—minus the sex. It's not all our fault. Our gay husbands who can't perform in bed with us try to compensate in other ways to be good husbands. And that's why so many times I hear from women, "We had the ideal marriage—except for the sex."

On the day that the husband comes to terms with himself enough to reveal the devastating news, the wife goes into a state of shock even if she's not really shocked. I often hear the words, "I didn't have a clue." It's hard to believe that a sexless marriage is not a clue, but I do understand this. With the lack of previous sexual experience that many women have, they will often buy into the lies and excuses passed along by their husbands. It is so easy to be blindsided when this news comes out when you just don't understand homosexuality.

While your husband has had the "luxury" of figuring out for years is now dumped in your lap to figures out in moments. I think all of us have the same initial reactions. They range from "He's confused," to "There must be a way to fix this." In fact, some women initially feel a tremendous sense of relief that it is "homosexuality" not "heterosexuality" that seems to be the problem. In their naïve minds, they believe that if they love their husbands "better," try harder, lose weight, clean better, become more nurturing, etc. etc., etc., he will come to his senses.

As the days, weeks, or months move on, we realize there's no fixing this broken situation, and we have to deal with the reality that our marriages, as we knew them, are over. For those couples who choose to stay together for whatever the reason, marriage will never be the same. All sorts of adjustments and compromises will be made to keep the marriage in tact. And I know women who are living this life. Are they happy? Not usually. But they weigh and measure their lives and cir-cumstances and make the decision to remain with their gay husbands.

The truth is, these women are still in their marriages because their husbands don't have the courage to do what's right and leave. They are more secure living within the confines of a straight marriage because they don't have the guts to live in the gay world. And chances are, these women will not have to deal with the issues of homosexuality with their children. These are the men who like to stay hidden in marriages fearful that their homosexuality will be exposed. They are not looking to make their life public, not even to their children. Let me add that most of these men love their wives on some level. There is a comfort level of acceptance in the relationship that keeps them there. Yes, the wife and family serve as a "shield" for some of these husbands, but they still feel love for their family.

But for the many men who leave their marriages because they have to be true to who they are, they need to find their place in a world that is new territory to them. In their quest to understand their identity, they venture out into unfamiliar territories hoping to find their level of comfort. In those early days, there is often sadness and depression on their part. I see it all the time. The gay world is not one that they can easily jump into and find a smooth road.

I compare it to people who are winning their freedom from an oppressive country. For instance, when refugees from communist countries came to America, they came here filled with hope and anxious anticipation for a better life. Their lives were so confined in their own countries that all they could dream about was the day when they would be free. They loved their country, but hated their lives under oppression. They believed that once they reached the shores of America, all of their past horrors would disappear and they would find utopia. They knew it would be a difficult challenge, but they were so excited by the thought of freedom, that nothing would stand in their way of seeking this new life.

The reality when they landed here was quite different than the dream they had. They were strangers in a strange land. They had to learn the language, the customs, and the habits. Americans knew that they were new immigrants here and often took advantage of that fact. They found themselves thrust into a world that was so different from the one they knew. It's not that they necessarily missed their country per se, but they missed the familiarity of all that they knew. When we feel a sense of abandonment, whether by choice or by force, all circumstances that were horrible as we lived them become romanticized and enhanced. We become nostalgic for the old days, even if we mentally "rework" what the old days were really like as a sort of mental safety net.

These new immigrants have great difficulty fitting into a society that is so different from the one they knew. Often they come here leaving their families behind and they long for the security and love of their family. It takes a long time to make the adjustment of culture, language, and personal interactions. During that transitional time, there is lots of pain and loneliness.

For neophytes in the gay community, this is how it is also. They know that they have been trapped in a world for their whole lives that is not their world. Although they have been able to live in it, it is not theirs. They love their wives and their children, but they are not feeling fulfilled. They know there is something missing that will never feel right as long as they stay there. They know they are gay, no matter how much they have tried to escape it. And now that the time has come to make the move, they feel the same sense of excitement and anticipation that the new immigrant feels. But in most cases, they also feel the same sense of hardship once they enter it.

The gay world for men who are newly coming out is filled with heartache and heartbreak. After coming out of a long-term "stable" relationship with a woman, these men of marriage are expecting to find a similar same-sex experience with a man. They are not even sure what their role is in the gay community. It is common for wives to comment on how their husbands' appearances are altered so greatly once they leave the home. Some of them change their whole look from coloring their hair to shaving their head bald. They start to dress differently, walk differently, talk differently and act differently.

I remember when my ex-husband first left me and started finding his way through this maze. On one of his early visits about four months after he left, I was appalled. He came dressed very feminine with a scarf around his neck. He came with a new friend he had made, and both of them looked like stereotypical "queens." His hand mannerisms and walk reflected a great sense of femininity. I was quite shocked and sickened. Where was the macho man that I had married who prided himself on his masculinity? Where did he go and how did this woman get inside this man? I was so upset when he left after a few hours thinking that I was glad my children were young enough not to remember that day.

My ex was struggling to find his way in the gay lifestyle. He didn't know where he belonged, and thankfully, he realized he didn't belong in that space. I would have had a very difficult time interacting with him if he would have stayed in that mode. His journey to find himself took a while. It wasn't an easy one, but in time he felt more of a level of comfort. I remember during that transitional year he would call me and ask me if we could try again. I knew he was speaking out of desperation because he wasn't adjusting to his new life. He missed the security and love that a marriage offered him even if he was miserable and felt trapped. The grass was looking greener now that he was on the other side.

In fairness to our gay husbands, most of them love us. Even when they leave us they love us. They don't love us the way we need to be loved because they are gay. But this doesn't negate the fact that they do love us to the best of their ability. Even though their love for us could never fulfill them to make them happy, it suddenly seems better than the rejection they are facing now that they are out in the gay community.

When gay married men enter this new world, it is often said that they are like "kids in a candy shop." This is true. Their eyes are wide open at all times looking at all the dangling goodies. For men who never spent time in the gay world or just had fleeting encounters, they try to make up for all of their suppressed years. Many enter the well-known side of the gay lifestyle, which usually starts out at gay bars and clubs. There they find whatever they are looking for when it comes to sex. Sex is a plentiful in these places and it is not uncommon to have a string of meaningless sexual experiences. But it's also a very superficial world built on fantasy, not reality. And that's why our husbands are often hurt early in the game. They are looking for love and stability in all the wrong places. We often joke that in the gay world, a week is a long-term relationship. Our husbands go into the gay world looking for straight values and they can't understand why it isn't happening.

Part of the reason is who they are looking for. Almost universally, when a gay man leaves a marriage and enters the gay world, he is looking for someone who is younger. My ex tells me it's because they are looking to recapture the youth and innocence that they never had a chance to enjoy when they were younger and living the straight life. I'm not sure if that's the only reason, but I'll buy into it because it sounds as logical as any other explanation. And so many of my gay male friends tell me that when they were young, they were looking for older men because it represented a sense of security that they couldn't find with guys their own age. So, I guess it's no wonder that these generational gap relationships are plentiful. Do they last? Rarely. And in most cases, they end with in a short amount of time.

In the beginning of this gay odyssey, while a man is exploring his new lifestyle, this becomes his obsession. He's an addict. The sugary candy is all that is on his mind. He loses sight of almost all of his past because he is trying to fit into his present. Women often ask me why their husbands are so obsessed with the gay sexual scene. Why do they have to have a string of sexual encounters? Why isn't one just enough to satisfy them? I explain it's like any other kind of addiction. They are always seeking the ultimate experience. It's like a drug addict who is seeking the ultimate high. No hit is ever enough because they are always thinking that the next one will take them to new heights of high. It's like the gambler who wins but has to put down the next bet, or the food addict who has a feast but before he's finished starts thinking about the next meal. That's the only way I can explain it to make it have any kind of relative meaning to those of us who just can't understand it.

That being said, maybe it can give you some insight into why the men whom we thought we knew so well become strangers in our midst. Maybe that will help you understand why during this metamorphosis, they change so drastically. Does it excuse their behavior? Of course not. Does it make us feel better now that we know this? Not really or necessarily. But at least it explains what is happening which is half the battle in knowing what to expect.

As the years go on, these men find their place in the gay world. Most of them develop stronger romantic relationships with men who are their peers once they have had their fill of casual sexual encounters. Some of these relationships last for a long period of time and there is a comparative sense of "straight stability." But I have also seen a sense of acceptance among many of these relationships that allow for outside sexual activity either agreeably or secretively. I and often hear from these men that sex and love have little to do with each other. They truly love their partners that they live with, and having sex with someone else doesn't negate that love. It's just sex, after all. It's the nature a man. Men were not meant to be monogamous. At least that's what these men tell me!

So when your husband closes the door when he is walking out, he is closing a chapter of his life. His life, as he knew it with you, will never be the same. He is about to enter the outer limits or twilight zone, but that's part of the design. You'll be hearing from him, trust me. Don't be surprised if he wants to come home after a short stint on the gay love boat, even to the point of threatening suicide which is not that uncommon. But don't be tricked into becoming a security blanket for his fears and difficulty in adjustment. Say "no" because otherwise you will have to relive his leaving all over again as soon as his confidence returns. It's hard enough to split up once. Don't put yourself through it again. He has no choice in being gay, but you have the choice to say no when he turns back in desperation.

One problem that faces all of us is the pressure we get from family members and friends to **"get over it"** when it comes to "recovery" from our marriages. Our loved ones, no matter how well meaning, can't understand why we are having such trouble doing this. Their intentions are good. They want us to get past the nightmare and move on to a happier state of mind. They see straight marriages ending in divorce all of the time and people seem to manage to start over again and find new relationships much more easily than we do.

I do get upset when I hear these stories of added additional pressure from women who are trying their best to move through the stages of anger and hurt but not at the pace that others expect of them. The end of a marriage is like the death of a loved one in many ways, and we all have to pass through the various stages of denial and anger before we can come to the point of acceptance. And acceptance for us is two fold— accepting the marriage is over and accepting the homosexuality of our husbands.

What other people don't realize is that there are numerous issues that we have to deal with after a marriage to a gay spouse ends. Some of these issues are unique and unlike those that women with straight husbands face. We have to figure out what to say to the children and when to tell them; we also have to decide what to tell family, friends, and co-workers. We live in a world where people still don't understand about a gay husband and fear the ridicule we will face from this ignorance. There are still many very ignorant people out there. Even in this day and age, people say, "What did you do to make him gay? After all, he wasn't gay when he married you."

We have to rebuild our own self-esteem, which has been sorely damaged through these marriages by not only feeling the failure of a marriage, but also wondering how much of a lie we were living. We have to rebuild our sense of trust within our own decision-making processes knowing that we walked blindly into a situation where we were so misled.

Most of us have lost or never had the feeling of what real intimacy means in a relationship. We have difficulty trusting men again and trusting our own ability not to walk into this situation one more time. And this is a genuine fear that many women express—"It happened to me once. How do I know the next man I get involved with won't be gay?" After all, why couldn't we tell the first time around? This is confirmed by the ignorance of others who insist that we "must have known but married him anyway because we thought we could change him."

There are other complications as well. There are those women who still feel some sense of responsibility for their husbands' homosexuality. They are convinced that they played some part in their husbands turning to men. That's because some gay husbands are cruel enough to say that to their wives rather than take the responsibility for the truth.

We have to deal with our own feelings of homophobia. Even if we were understanding of homosexuality in general terms, it took a whole new meaning when it entered our marriages and ruined our hopes and dreams for our futures with our husbands. We have to deal with our own feelings about our husbands bringing lovers into the lives of our children and how that will affect our children emotionally. We have to fear how other people will treat our children if they find out. And of course, we now have to contend with the possibility that our children will be gay because this is a new reality.

Certainly straight marriages that end go through emotional upset and turmoil. We have to go through those same problems, such as single parenthood, financial problems, selling the home, and legal tangles. But in addition, we are forced to deal with all the additional issues stated above. This is a double whammy that just doesn't end when a marriage ends.

What saddens me are the dozens of letters I receive each week from women who just can't work their way through the maze of emotional complications that they are left with not only during the marriage, but also after the marriage. This is a process that takes time. But without going through a number of steps, it will take much longer or just leave wounds that will not heal.

Women with gay husbands have to go through a grieving and recovery period much like others who have to deal with the death of a loved one. The noted therapist Elizabeth Kubler Ross established the five stages of mourning when it comes to death and dying. I have applied these same stages to the context of those of you who are mourning your marriages to your gay husbands to try to give you a better understanding. I believe that understanding these stages will help you through this difficult period and give you some insight of what emotional turmoil to expect in the days, months or years ahead.

STAGE ONE – DENIAL AND SHOCK

The first stage that every woman goes through after learning about her husband's homosexuality is denial. You can't believe this is happening. If you fall upon the information on your own, you are sure that what you have found is not true. You look for reasons to help keep you in denial. You refuse to believe the evidence, even if it is staring you right in the face. When you confront your husband with your suspicions and he says "No," and has some logical explanation, you feel a sense of relief because it is much easier to live not believing this news. For those of you who are fortunate enough to have a husband who is truthful, you still go through denial. You tell him, "You must be mistaken," or "This is just a phase—you'll get over it." The magnitude of this revelation is just too difficult for you to

70

comprehend. Even when your husband leaves, you still think, and in some cases hope that he will "wake up" and realize that this **"gay thing"** is crazy and he'll come back to his loving wife and secure marriage. When you are in denial, it means that your mind is not able to face the enormity of the problem and this is a natural defense against the news.

We keep denying the truth because it serves as a defensive measure against the impact of the trauma. Once we are able to absorb the truth, we go through a period of "shock." I remember this stage quite vividly when I was going through my own mourning period. This is when I was walking around on two different planes. Part of me was physically functioning and mechanically doing the day-to-day living chores. The mental part of me was stuck as if in shock, not processing much at all. I would hear the world around me, but block it out. I felt as if I was "existing," but not living. I really didn't have emotional highs or lows because I wasn't dealing with my emotions at all. I just kept moving doing what I had to do to get through the day, but I wasn't mentally or emotionally functioning.

It is much easier for women who have husbands who admit the truth to get past this stage because they now know what they are dealing with. As much as the truth hurts, it is at least the truth, and you can move through these stages more quickly knowing what you are facing. For those of you who have the misfortune of being married to men who are still in denial themselves or just afraid to tell you the truth, plan to remain in this stage much longer. You bounce back and forth between denial and shock. And you want to believe so strongly that this problem will go away. When your husbands show you renewed spurts of love and attention after feeling guilty or fearing that you are learning the truth, it is easy to lull yourselves back into the net of false security. But once you suspect, the thoughts never quite go away, even when you try to bury them deep into your subconscious. They are like little gnats, flying overhead like pesky little bugs that you can't swat away more than momentarily.

Some women are so afraid asking their husbands for the truth that they just keep piling up the evidence waiting for the "right time" for the confrontation. This is their way of working through their husbands' anticipated denial in case the sound of **"No way"** comes out of the mouths of their husbands when the question is finally asked. As long as you are stockpiling evidence as confirmation for yourself, this is fine. Some of you will never hear the true confession no matter what proof you show your husbands, and the evidence will be all that you have to go on. (Gut feelings only go so far!) But there comes a time when you have to face your husbands with the facts that you have uncovered, and by this point, you should be mentally prepared to deal with the situation regardless of his explanations.

STAGE TWO – ANGER AND RESENTMENT

After passing through the denial stage, you move into anger. You continually question, *"How could he have done this to me?"* *"Why didn't he tell me this before he married me?"* *"He really didn't love me, he used me."* *"Doesn't he care about the children and how this will affect their lives?"* It is very natural to be angry after realizing that your husband is gay. You feel a sense of betrayal because you were lied to. Even if the lie wasn't intentional, and even if your husband hadn't come to terms with his homosexuality prior to marriage, he certainly knew he was having these feelings long before he told you about it. You thought that your marriage was based on basic truths that did not include homosexuality. Now you discover a problem that is incomprehensible and it has permeated the entirety of your lives.

You are angry and you vacillate where we should place the blame. You blame your husband first for betraying you. You blame yourself for not being smart enough to see the truth. You blame friends and family members who come to you later and tell you that they suspected your husband during the marriage but were afraid to say anything. You blame your husband's parents for "making" him this way. After all, he had a very domineering mother or passive father that must have created this problem. If he has a lover, you blame the lover for "turning" him this way when he wasn't this way to start with. You blame God, all homosexuals, and anything or anyone else available. Some women believe that if they are angry enough, the problem will vanish as if they can chase it away by yelling it away. But it doesn't go away no matter how hard you wish it or pray it away.

When women go through the anger stage, it is important to be able to express this anger to others and find support. It always hurts me when I find women who have been harboring their anger for years internally, afraid to express it to anyone. The anger must be dealt with because otherwise you become stuck in this phase and never move ahead. First you may feel irrational anger placing the blame everywhere it doesn't belong, and that is okay. But it is important to start dealing with the anger and direct it appropriately and rationally. If not, you will find yourself becoming bitter and looking at life through distorted perceptions.

My friend, Dina Hamer, put a very positive spin on the anger stage. She feels that anger is important because it means that you are standing up and fighting for yourself. To quote Dina:

"Initial anger is a mandatory step towards recovery, as it liberates one from the earlier stages of shock, denial, internalization, and self blame. By admitting anger, one engages in reality testing and shifts the blame from one self to the real cause and beyond. It implies a regaining of control as opposed to passive acceptance and inactivity. That said, anger will trigger awareness which ultimately will be the tool for self-actualization and rebuilding; however, remaining in the anger mode indefinitely can ultimately prove to be equally self-destructive. As with any emotional stage of grief, it should be transitory and viewed as a catalyst towards the next step in growth - regaining oneself."

Anger is the first step of moving ahead. I strongly agree with Dina's statement and know how important it is go through this stage because it means that you are out of the denial stage and moving forward. Thank you, Dina, for sharing your eloquence with our readers.

STAGE THREE – BARGAINING

It is not unusual for you to start bargaining with your husband and yourself. *"If only I can be a better wife, maybe you won't feel this need for someone else." "If only I can lose weight and be more attractive, you will find yourself attracted to me as much as you did when you married me."* You are so afraid of losing what you had or what you thought you had that you try every *"If only"* as a bargaining chip. You think that if you can change yourself, you will change your husband's homosexuality. Of course, no amount of your greatest efforts will ever change his desires, but that doesn't stop you from trying, especially when you can't understand how after 10, 20, or 30 years of what you thought was a successful marriage, your husband has these needs.

Other women start bargaining to keep their marriages together, coming up with **"I can live with that"** plans that seldom work. *"If you can satisfy your urges by looking at pictures or movies, I can live with that." "If you slip out once every six months and satisfy your urges and I never find out, I can live with that." "If you promise never to cheat on me, I can live with that."* Sometimes, a husband will agree to anything because he also doesn't want to leave the marriage. He will give you his personal assurances that he will never stray, and you are eager to accept this as fact. But every time he walks through the door ten minutes late, you start to wonder where he's been. Living under a cloak of suspicion for years to come is very debilitating to your sense of self-worth. Eventually, your husband will act on his natural urges and you have to face that fact. He is gay and he needs a man to make him feel fulfilled in his life. It doesn't mean that he doesn't love you in his own way; it just means that you can never totally fulfill his needs no matter what you do.

There are those of you who are bargaining with the term *"bisexuality."* You feel relieved to hear this term because it gives you a very false sense of hope. It sounds much more pleasant than *"gay"* and makes you think that your husband can continue living with you exclusively. Even if he has occasional urges for men, you are sure that he can suppress them. After all, doesn't *"bisexual"* mean that he can be happy either way? And he chose to be happy with you. Well, ladies, this doesn't work. It may make life more palatable temporarily, but your husband's needs for men won't disappear. In time, the desire will be so strong that when the opportunity arises, he will take advantage of it.

The problem with prolonged bargaining is that it keeps destroying your own sense of self-esteem. What you are really feeling is that you are the failure in the marriage, not your husband. You are hoping that if you can change yourself enough, whether it is through appearance, personality, or thinking, your husband will be able to change himself and not have gay desires anymore. This just prolongs the sense of finality.

STAGE FOUR – WITHDRAWAL AND DEPRESSION

After you realize that nothing can change your husband's homosexuality, you often go through a period of withdrawal. This is when you isolate yourself from family and friends because you are going through your own depression. You are thinking about how your future will drastically change from all the dreams and plans you had. You are able to face reality now and think about the obstacles that stand in front of you. For many of you, this means single parenthood and financial instability. You are frightened of the unknown and what lies ahead of you. Some of you have lost the confidence and trust in your own judgment and fear that you can't survive on your own.

For those women whose husbands have no intention of leaving the relationship, you feel trapped as if there is no way out. Some of you are so mentally beaten down that you have accepted this marriage as your own personal **life sentence**, or shall I say, **death sentence**. This throws you into a deeper sense of depression and causes you to lose perspective of life. There is always a way out of your marriage even if it can't happen at this minute. You can only reach physical freedom if after you achieve mental freedom. That applies to any bad relationship.

No matter how much you think that you can't make it on your own in life, this is never the case. All of us were single before we married and somehow making it through life before we met our husbands. Your situations may have been altered through children, but you can still create a positive and fulfilling life for yourself even though it may be financially difficult. I know because I was there. I was a strong woman before my marriage who was transformed into a person unknown to those around me and even myself as each layer of confidence was stripped away. I used to fantasize about killing my husband because I didn't believe there was any other way to remove the reigns around my neck that seemed to be strangling me anytime I tried to make a move. Telling this to you is perhaps admitting my lowest point during the marriage and what *hopelessness* drives us to.

The difference between this stage for women with gay husbands versus the mourning of a loved one who dies is the fact that there is no finality to it. In the grieving process of the death of a loved one, you can look back at your past and reflect and remember him with wonderful memories. With a gay husband, you are forced to deal with a whole extra set of problems that you were not planning on, and in many cases, are not accepting of. You have to sift through your feelings of betrayal. You have to unravel your own feelings of blame and inadequacy. You have to work with the issue of raising the children knowing that your husband has a lifestyle that you may not be comfortable with or want your children to be exposed to. You have to work on all of your personal issues that have gone haywire during your marriage such as self-esteem, sexual esteem, and trust in your judgment. Many of you now become part of the single-parent world and have to learn how to juggle your time and finances. While your husband seems to be enjoying his new life, you are often resentful that he often seems not only adjusted to his new life, and is, in fact enjoying his new freedom and new sexuality. It hurts like hell because we feel our world has come crashing down while his world is moving ahead. This is not to say that some gay husbands aren't suffering too, but that doesn't make us feel much better. On their part, they just don't seem to be suffering as much—or as some wives feel-- enough.

To deal with the depression, many women start taking antidepressants looking for a way to numb the pain. Actually, some of these women have been taking medication for a while just to cope with the hardships in their marriage. This may suppress the anxiety and hurt temporarily, but it also suppresses the ability to deal with the situation in the long run. That's why it's so important to have support while you are going through this stage. And just when you think that you are making great strides, you may backslide into feeling depressed again. All of us move at different paces—some quickly, some slowly. There are so many variables such as the time in the marriage, the condition the marriage was in before the news, the support the husband gives when he leaves, family influences, and outside support. It doesn't matter how quickly or slowly you are moving ahead—as long as you are moving and not getting repeatedly stuck in a bad space.

STAGE FIVE – ACCEPTANCE

This is the last stage of the grieving process. After you understand that your husband's homosexuality and the failure of your marriage were in no way your fault, you are able to start moving on emotionally and accept that your life has changed. For some of you who were in emotionally abusive marriages, this change is definitely for the best. For others who were in unfulfilling marriages and couldn't understand why there was always something missing even though we couldn't pinpoint the cause, the change is also positive. But there are also those women who felt that they had wonderful marriages and can't understand what changed. Acceptance for these women sometimes takes longer because they keep questioning why a relationship that seemed so satisfying to both of them really wasn't that satisfying to their husbands. These women have the most difficult time because they were happy in their marriages and would have stayed there forever. There is no relief on their part—only sadness for a longer period of time.

Regardless of what your situation is, you will go through these stages in a similar way. And you need to also realize that just when you think you're past one stage and moving into the next, you can go back and forth. The anger and resentment may come back again when you think you've dealt with it. That's because the relationship isn't over when you have children. Children tie people together for life. When you have serious differences in how you want to raise your children or if your husband is not meeting up to his parenting duties and financial responsibilities, your anger will no doubt surface again. This is normal in all relationships that end, not just straight/gay ones.

Dina (Hamer) recently sent me an article on death and dying that spurred me on to write this one. It was in the context of losing a love one and the grieving process. Unfortunately, I couldn't identify the author of the article to give him/her credit for this next statement. But I believe in our context it definitely does apply and is so important.

The article stated that there is one more stage that people can go through to help the healing process, and that is **OUTREACH.** By reaching out to others who are in the initial phases of grieving and offering empathetic listening, you can create great friendships and camaraderie. Helping others who are going through this situation with support helps give reassurance that you are on the way to healing and moving ahead. No one can understand the emotional turmoil we face better than someone who has lived through it. No matter how different we may be in age, location, religion, culture, education, finances, and professions, this tragedy breaks through all barriers and bonds us together. Women who feel so isolated and alone as if they are the only ones in the world who are suffering with this problem now see that they are not an oddity, but rather part of a group of millions. By reaching out and sharing, you are able to give hope to other women that life can go on and be fulfilling and happy again.

I have been blessed to meet some wonderful women who do outreach to others going through this hardship. As they, themselves, are healing, they reach out to others to help them through this process We have the greatest women in our on-line support group who are there to listen and share with everyone who needs support. If you are ever in need of feeling understood and cared about, join us on a Tuesday, Thursday or Sunday evening and you will feel a new sense of kinship and positive feelings. Email me at Bonkaye@aol.com for more information.

Although understanding the stages that women go through after they learn about homosexuality is the first step, there are steps to take that can make the healing easier. In some ways, going through recovery from your gay husband is similar to other addiction recoveries. For that reason, I have adapted the traditional 12-step recovery program that people use for recovery of alcohol, drugs, overeating, and co-dependency and revised them to what I call the "*12 Step Gay Husband*

Recovery (GHR)." For those of you who are stuck in a place or space that you need to move out of, hopefully this will help you.

THE TWELVE STEPS TO
<u>GAY HUSBAND RECOVERY (GHR)</u>

1. You admit that your husband is gay, and you are powerless to change his homosexuality. You accept that you had no responsibility in "turning" your husband gay, and he has no choice in being gay. You also accept that your marriage has become unmanageable living with homosexuality.

a. The first step in working towards recovery is to admit those words that are so difficult and painful to say—"**My husband is gay.**" You have to accept this as the beginning premise and not look to find excuses or lull yourself into a false state of security by saying the word, "**bisexual.**"

b. Once you can accept that your husband is gay, you must then understand and believe that you are in no way responsible for this. Your husband was gay long before you met him even if he couldn't understand this himself. You in no way brought this out in him or caused him to change into this. You had no influence one way or the other on when his need to act on his homosexuality would surface. There is nothing you could have done to stop this from occurring.

c. You realize that your marriage is in turmoil because your husband is gay, not because you failed as a wife. Even if there are numerous other problems in the marriage, they are all tied in to this basic fact.

2. You believe that once you turn for help for yourself, you can restore yourself to sanity.

You cannot change your husband, and no matter what you do to improve your beauty, intellect, or personality. *it will not make a difference*. You must turn to others who can lend help and support to understand how and why this happens so you can start thinking clearly and rationally. You need to rebuild your self-esteem and sense of self-worth so that you can start thinking ahead to the real solutions that are necessary. **<u>You do not need to waste time or money going for family counseling to try to make this marriage work</u>.** When you are living with a gay man, the bottom line is he will always have the physical and/or emotional need to be with men. This is not something that can change if you both go for marriage counseling together. Instead, go for counseling yourself to work on regaining the emotional strength you need to cope with in the marriage until you are able to move out of it.

3. Make a decision to take back your own life, which has somehow been misplaced through your marriage.

Throughout your marriage, you have focused on your husband instead of yourself. This is for the most part because you have spent your time trying to please him because he doesn't seem fulfilled. You personalize this as your failure and so you try that much harder to be a "better wife." It is not surprising if you have lost sight of who you are or who you were before the marriage. You have somehow misplaced your own life and aspirations while trying to make yourself into someone whom your husband can love better. It is now time to start focusing on you and what your hopes were prior to the time of the marriage. You did have a life before your husband as well as dreams and goals. It's time to revisit that period of your life.

If you married at a young age, you may have never had time to work on personal goals. View this as an opportunity to sit down and dream about the life you want. Mentally visualize yourself in a place where there is happiness based upon trust and truth rather than chaos, confusion, and lies.

4. Make a search of personal inventory to see what it is within yourself that has allowed you to lose sight of your own identity and who you were before your marriage.

It is common to get off track while trying desperately to make your marriage succeed. Now it is time to do some personal inventory to see why you have allowed yourself to regress to the low emotional state you are in. What is it within you that keeps you hanging on to this marriage long after it should be over? What insecurities and fears are you facing? Living with a gay husband brings about a number of common emotional problems such as lowering or loss of personal self-esteem, loss of sexual self-esteem, and feelings of hopelessness.

You need to focus on a major issue that will haunt you for the rest of your life unless you deal with it upfront—namely, **TRUST.** You have lost the ability to trust your own judgment. You must learn to trust your own instincts again and not allow a mistake beyond your control to jade your ability to make future decisions. You must first trust that you were a worthy woman prior to your marriage. You were able to think rationally before you met your husband. But after living in an "Alice in Wonderland Upside Down World" existence over a period of time, you start looking at life through distorted mirrors which distort your thoughts, which increase through living a lie. Once the lie is exposed, it is time for you to start examining how that lie impacted on your important decisions or fear of making important decisions.

When going through the step of taking personal inventory, start making a list of all of the qualities you have. Start recognizing your wonderful strengths and traits that have somehow been minimized in the shadow of your husband's problem. Start thinking about how those positives would have been accentuated if you had been married to someone who could have been a real husband to you by being encouraging and supportive rather than finding fault with you because he was frustrated living his lie.

5. Admit to yourself and to others what the real problem is in the marriage—your husband's homosexuality—and not look to place the blame on yourself.

Until you can internally believe that your husband's homosexuality is not your fault, it is impossible to move on. You need to understand and accept that you were not "stupid" walking into this marriage or even naïve. You were uninformed, inexperienced, and lacking the knowledge of understanding homosexuality. You thought that gay men were attracted to the same sex relationships, not relationships with straight women. Even if you knew about past gay encounters in your husband's life or suspected there had been homosexual contact, you believed in all good faith that your husband had "chosen" to change and you accepted his explanation when he told you this. Remember, the overwhelming majority of women who marry gay men had no idea whatsoever about this prior to the marriage. Those who had any suspicion or knowledge didn't understand that homosexuality was not just an adolescent encounter or fantasy. For the handful or women who went knowingly into the marriage with a gay husband, you believed in your heart that if your husband loved you enough, he would change. Stop punishing yourself by thinking that you didn't see the "**un-obvious**" signs.

6. You are ready to develop a mental plan for a positive future and believe that life can become rewarding and fulfilling after your marriage.

In order to regain hope, you must believe that there can be life after your marriage. Some women don't believe that this is possible and view their marriages as a life sentence. This is not the case. Even if you can't leave your marriage at this moment, you can start to plan for a positive future regardless of your age. Stop putting up negative roadblocks such as, "I can't financially support myself," or "I'm out of shape," or "I'm too old to start over." These are self-defeating messages which allow you to stay "stuck" where you are. All of the money in the world can't buy your happiness. It doesn't make sense to stay emotionally dead just to keep a roof over your head. You can put your life back together in time as long as you start believing in yourself. It may take you a year or five years, but the bottom line is that if you want it, it will happen.

Part of developing a mental plan is realizing that you may be taking anti-depressants because you are depressed living in your marriage. So many women are coping in their marriages or after their marriages this way. If your depression is due to the marriage, antidepressants will numb the pain as well as other feelings. However, medication can also stop you from dealing with your feelings which is essential if you expect to move ahead to a produce and happier life. If you are taking medication as a result of your depression from your marriage, realize that you need to put limits on how long you can suppress your emotions. Medication doesn't change the situation that your husband is gay, nor will it make you any happier living in a marriage with a gay man.

7. You are willing to accept you have your own insecurities and low self-esteem issues and need to start working to change them.

Women in these marriages are often plagued with insecurities and low self-esteem. This is because marriage to a gay man is an unnatural state of marriage to live in. Staying in a marriage void of passion and intimacy is also an unnatural state of marriage no matter how nice a partner is. If you wanted only friendship, you didn't need to get married. You wanted a husband and a complete marriage that includes physical intimacy. Too many women end up "redefining" marriage justifying that there's all different kinds of relationships. This thinking may make you feel better temporarily, but certainly not in the long run.

Living daily knowing that your husband desires a man over you strips away your sense of self-esteem one layer at a time. It is a slow process that erodes your mental state over time, not all at once. When you don't know that the problem is homosexuality, the feelings of personal rejection are even worse because you believe that you are doing something wrong in the marriage.

Gay husbands who won't be honest will often say that "you" have the problem, not them. They claim they are happy because they can't come to terms with their truth and would rather continue living their lie. They make you start believing that you are the cause of your own unhappiness because they claim to be "happy." This is why so many women invest so much time and money going for therapy to help a problem that they don't even know exists.

I know women who have gone to such extremes as developing eating disorders, investing in surgery including breasts implants, gastric bypasses, and liposuction, and even going to sex therapists in hopes of getting their gay husbands to desire them more. They don't understand how their husbands loved them enough to marry them but now won't continue to desire them in the bedroom. They don't understand that no matter what they do, they can't make themselves attractive or more desirable to their gay husbands because they are not men.

8. Make a list of all aspects of your life that have been altered through the marriage and look for ways to mend them.

I know that having a gay husband alters the lives of most women. When you live in a state of constantly trying to please your husband, you lose sight of what you can achieve for yourself. Some women have never received the emotional support or encouragement from their husbands and have given up on their own dreams. In our desperation to keep the "status quo," we have freeze on the idea of education, employment, and socialization.

It is important to start focusing on goals that will help you build or rebuild yourself. It is time to start mapping out a game plan on how you can achieve these goals whether you are with your husband or no longer with him. When I lived with my gay husband, I became a prisoner of my own insecurities like many of you have. We are afraid to walk away from the house for fear of what will be going on in our absence. This leaves us in a state of paralyzation, afraid to make a move in any direction, including a positive direction. We stop socializing with friends and family; we put any plans of improving ourselves through education or employment on hold; we literally become locked up in our own fears of what will happen if we walk out the door.

I wasted so much valuable time not doing for me because I was afraid of what he would be doing for him if I left the home. You must accept the fact that you cannot be a 24-hour guard against his homosexuality. You cannot stop him from acting on his needs just by surrounding him every moment. He will find ways to do what he needs to do regardless of how hard you try to stop in. And in doing so, you are only stopping yourself from moving ahead. Start focusing on you because otherwise you will be wasting years of your life that could be fulfilling and productive.

9. Make contact with other people however you have to in order to feel connected rather than isolated and alone. You must not be afraid to seek out help wherever you can even it is against the wishes of your gay husband.

You cannot put your husband's need for privacy and discretion ahead of your need for support and help. You must understand why you keep putting his need for secrecy before your need for sanity.

It is amazing how ashamed so many women feel when it comes to discussing this subject with family members, friends, co-workers, or medical professionals. This is a subject that has been kept quiet for so long because we are afraid of how others will judge us. Our greatest fear is that people will believe that we are the cause of our husband's homosexuality. On some level we still internalize that this is our fault and haven't accepted that our husbands were gay when we married them. Some women who finally come to terms with this fact continue to blame themselves and feel that these were suppressed feelings in their husbands that they have somehow triggered by not being good enough wives.

When we seal ourselves off from others and deal with these thoughts alone, we feel an even greater sense of isolation and failure. In order to recover, you must be willing to share this news with others and seek support. Once you can say the words, "My husband is gay," to someone, it is a major step forward in finding personal independence.

10. You are willing to confront your gay husband on any issues and not be afraid that you are going to do more damage than has already been done.

When you suspect that your husband is gay, or in some cases, have proof that your husband is involved with gay activities such as porno, websites, emails, etc., it is important for you to confront him with your suspicions and findings. This is not an easy thing to do, but carrying this burden yourself is self-defeating. You need to let him know as soon as possible why you suspect there is a problem. If he denies this, or tells you that you are crazy, don't give up. In some cases he will be very defensive and angry, but that should not be the basis of your shutting down. In some cases he may be in denial, but you must continue to tell him about your feelings in hopes that he will do the right thing.

You need to accept that this is a problem that will not go away no matter how hard both of you wish it away. In many cases, your husband fears telling you the truth because he is scared that you will have the confirmation you need to walk away or use it as ammunition against him. His fears will often keep him from admitting the truth to you. Don't "give up," "shut-up," or "shut-down."

11. Seek answers through support and professional help so that you can ease your knowledge that will give you the courage to change your life. You will explore all avenues that will result in your personal independence.

Finding out that your husband is gay is one of the worst experiences a woman can have. There is no way that you can expect to recover from this problem alone. You need help and support to help guide you through the difficult days ahead. There is no shame in going for help. In fact, now that you know that there is help and support, the shame is in not going for it. Find help that works for you in a meaningful way. Just like all therapists are not for you, not all groups claiming to be "support" groups are the right ones for you. If you are not comfortable with the support being given by various organizations, keep searching until you find the right one. In time, you will find help that is of the comfort level you need.

12. Having a new insight and education as a result of these steps, you try to carry this message to others who need to understand what your situation is about. You also try to extend yourself to others crying out for help who are lost and confused.

An excellent way to work through the healing process is to support others who are going through the same problem that you are. First, it gives comfort to others who are just starting on this path. Next, it helps you to know that there are others out there in the same situation so you don't feel isolated or alone. This will help you in your personal journey to *Gay Husband Recovery.*

The important thing is to keep moving ahead. Realize that this is a process that takes time and doesn't happen overnight. In time and with help, you will reach your goal of rebuilding your self-esteem and self-worth. Then it is time to step away from this period of your life and move on to a new part where positive self-discovery will bring you the happiness you seek and deserve.

Remember, as with any recovery program, you have to work these steps daily. You have to make them part of your internal belief system and look at them regularly to reassure yourself that you are on track. Any time you feel yourself slipping back instead of forward, read them over. You can and will recover!

Fears We Face—
Thinking the Unthinkable

There are a number of fears that we face when we learn that our husbands are gay. This is so natural because we are facing not only the impending doom of our hopes and dreams, but also now have to wade into unfamiliar territories which we never anticipated. Gay is no longer the funny guy in the movies or television who we laugh with or in some cases laugh at. Gay is now a terrifying force that has entered our personal lives, uninvited, and there's no way to say "Go away—I don't want you here."

When many women first write to me with their stories of devastation, some of them start thinking about every frightening thought that passes through their minds. Some of these fears are based on the dark side of gay life that are too visible to the general public. They don't represent the lives of most gay people, but it's what we see, just like the stereotypes are what we see that represent gay.

Each time I receive a letter expressing these thoughts, I remember back to the days when I first learned about my gay husband. Twenty years ago there was very limited information or resources to turn to. I had to live with my fears much longer than women today who can get answers more quickly thanks to the computer and the much larger public network of straight spouses.

I will discuss some of the most prevalent fears that women face. Some of these were discussed in my newsletters or touched on in my book, "*The Gay Husband Checklist for Women Who Wonder.*" I will expand upon them here.

The most important thing to realize is that some of the fears that we have are what I call **"IRRATIONAL FEARS."** These are fears that are based on people's false perceptions of gay. This kind of fear is dangerous to you and your children because it can create splits in family unity which are so important when a marriage ends. Your husband's homosexuality should not be the cause of alienation from your children. It's an issue of responsibility.

These questions are a compilation of the ones that women most frequently ask and have the most difficult time working through.

Q. If my husband is gay, will my children be gay?
A. It's possible. I was scared for years. I believe that gay is genetic, not a choice or learned behavior, and I know that genes can be passed on to children. In the 1980's as I met a greater number of families and started calculating multiple homosexual members of the immediate or extended family, I began to see a pattern that really alarmed me. *No one wants to have a homosexual child.* That is not a homophobic statement at all, but rather one based on a mother's love for her child. We all know how difficult it is to be gay in our society, and we don't want our children to have to face those hardships. However, recognizing that this was possible, I raised my children in an environment of positive feelings about homosexuality from a young age.

I corrected them when they would repeat derogatory statements they heard from friends, classmates, teachers, neighbors, and even television. I was honest about my friends who were openly gay and allowed them to serve as role models long before they knew about their father's homosexuality. I emphasized that people had no choice in their sexuality any more than they had a choice in their color, height, or eye color. Just because people were different, it didn't make them wrong or bad. I did this because I knew there was a greater chance of one or both of my children being gay because their father was

91

gay. And, I later learned that my ex-husband's birth father was "bisexual." The fact that Michael had never met him because he was adopted by extended family members at birth was further proof to me that gay is genetic vs. learned behavior.

As things turned out, our daughter, who passed away in April of 2002 at the age of 22, was a lesbian. When I discovered this three years before her death, I cried. No matter how much you prepare yourself for this possibility, you still cry when it becomes a reality. And when I finished crying, I hugged her and told her that I didn't care—and I didn't. My daughter told me that thanks to my attitude, she was able to accept who she was without running away from it and hiding like her father felt he had to do. She was comfortable with her sexuality. For that, I am grateful. I know all of the confusion and pain her father lived with for years trying to accepting himself. I felt good about that. Ironically, it was much easier for me to accept my daughter's homosexuality than it was for her father to accept it. And, her father was extremely defensive and angry if I brought up the fact that this is genetic, as if I was blaming him. There is no blame here, nor do I hold him responsible. But I know there is a part of him that feels responsible even though there is no blame intended.

I have spoken to so many women who have experienced one or more of their children being gay or struggling with accepting their homosexuality. I know that it is heartbreaking, but don't let this be a barrier between you and your child. By now you should understand that homosexuality is not a choice that anyone would consciously make. There are no choices when it comes to this. Love your child without letting this become an issue, otherwise you will both lose out. And in case this is a fear that becomes your reality as it did mine, stop the negative gay talk in front of your children lest they get the message that there is something wrong with them that will stop you from loving them if they are gay.

One last word on the subject of children. Many of us worry about our sons being gay without any thought at all about our daughters. The gender of the child has no bearing on the sexuality of the child. It's our natural tendency to think that gay husband could produce a gay son, but it is just as possible to produce a gay daughter. I mention this because it is important to accept that possibility so you learn how to address the issue of homosexuality with your daughters. Negative comments about gay to your girls may cause them to go through the same hardships of coming out as it would be for your sons. It is vital to let your female gendered children know that gay is okay so if this turns out to be their case, they do not grow up with feelings of hatred for who they are or fear living a happy, open life with their family–especially you.

I have seen so many families torn apart by the news of their children's homosexuality. Too many years are wasted because children can't deal with their parents' discomfort. To let homosexuality block your love for a child is totally ludicrous. There are many support groups in every area for parents with gay children. Do yourself a favor and join one if you have a hard time accepting this situation.

I feel proud of myself when I think about my own acceptance of my daughter's lesbianism. I always accepted her girlfriends as if they were my own daughters. I never felt embarrassed when she would hug or kiss them in front of me. It took some mind adjusting, but it was worth it to know that my daughter felt comfortable instead of isolated. The years I had with my daughter were cut down in her early adulthood. I can always look back knowing that she loved me because she knew how much I loved her and accepted her for who she was without having to try to change her.

Q. Can my child's sexuality be influenced if she/he spends time with his/her father and sees his lifestyle?

A. Absolutely not. Gay is not something that can be influenced when it comes to a person's sexuality. No one can "become" gay by hanging around gay people. Sexuality does not "rub off" on children. It can influence their opinions in either a positive or negative way about homosexuality, but it doesn't "turn them gay."

I find it so sad when I receive letters from time to time from women who have this terrible fear and for that reason, do their best to keep their children out of the reach of the gay father. This certainly can't help the situation and in fact, only worsens it. A child needs a father, and sexuality shouldn't be the issue. Responsible parenting should be the only concern. That being said (again), a gay father also has the responsibility to be sensitive to a child's feelings. If a child is uncomfortable being in a gay environment such as parties, picnics, social gatherings, etc., that should be the first consideration. Also, it isn't surprising that a child will feel uncomfortable with the father's lifestyle, especially during adolescence. No matter how much a child loves a father, it doesn't mean he or she is going to be comfortable with homosexuality through those difficult years.

Keep in mind that a child from a gay father is going to go through the natural fear that he/she will be gay, especially during adolescence when sexuality is so confusing. In addition to all of the other difficulties teenagers go through, this is just one more. As a result of these fears, they may act out differently than other teens. I have seen girls become promiscuous with guys just to prove that they aren't gay. My own daughter had her share of male sexual experiences prior to the time of coming to terms with herself. And guess what—she enjoyed those experiences. When you're young, your raging hormones are easy to satisfy. She just knew that her growing attraction to women was overtaking her desire for men. By the time she was 19, she was sure what side of the fence she was on. She never looked back after her discovery. She knew she wasn't "bisexual." She enjoyed women and that's who she was.

Yes, life would be so much easier for gay people if they could comes to terms with their sexuality this early in the course of life. But unfortunately, when you are trying to escape who you are, it's not easy at all. It's a struggle that often ends in disaster because of lack of family support. The end result—they get married to women like us and have to drag this journey out far too long.

Q. Do I have to worry about my gay husband being around my son? I read stories about some gay men liking younger boys and it scares me. And what about his gay friends? Will they go after my son?

A. I understand this fear. It comes from the darkest side of the horror stories that we hear when learning about homosexuality. I think much of this fear comes from the fact that our own husbands or ex-husbands are fixated on younger men. But it's ironic how we don't fear for our daughters when we are married to straight men. The thought of incest would never cross our minds, even though there are a far greater number of father-daughter incestuous relationships than there are gay father-son concerns. I won't say that this doesn't happen or can't happen, but I certainly wouldn't worry about this happening. This is a very irrational fear. Just because a person is gay doesn't mean that he is a child molester. It is so important to be able to differentiate between homosexuals and pedophiles.

Homosexuals often get the bum rap of being pedophiles, which is very disturbing to me. Pedophiles prey on innocent children, male and female, without much differentiation on whom they victimize. Even within the realm of pedophilia, there are many different kinds of child molesters, which make the situation even more complex. However, it is not unusual for gay men to like guys who are much younger than they are.

We feel this sense of discomfort when we find many of our husbands going after or out with younger men once they come out. This certainly does seem to be a common trend with gay men, especially when they come out at a later age. I have no concrete answer on why this happens, just numerous theories formed from the answers I've received from the gay men that I discuss this with, including my own ex-husband. Some say it's because they are recapturing their own youth; others say they are finally being able to act on the attraction they've had since they were that age but never had the chance to act on it.

Although the following statement will offend the sensitivities of some of my gay friends, I'll risk it. The value system of gay men differs from the value system of straight women when it comes to acceptance of having sexual relations with younger men in their teenage years. What would be totally unacceptable for us to accept as proper conduct is quite acceptable within the gay way of thinking. I am not sure where gay men draw the line of acceptable ages for pursing young men. However, I don't think that many gay men would object to a man at any age having sexual encounters with teenagers who are 17 or 18. The concern we all have is where does the line stop? Is 16 okay? Is 15 or 14? 13? There are some very shaky grounds when we speak about this.

As wives or ex-wives, the thought of our husbands being with young men whom we see as teenagers is a repulsive thought. We would feel a sense of repulsion if our husbands were straight and pursing 17-year-old girls, so it's not just a gay issue. However, we are so devastated by the imagery of our husbands with other men, that the thought of them being with younger men still in their teens is far more discomforting to us. This added to the fact that this is not only acceptable but also common behavior within the gay community is what is so upsetting to us. The explanation that these young men are seeking older men because it represents a sense of security, experience, and stability doesn't comfort us at all. We are still sickened at the visualization.

We are also worried about our own sons. It's a common fear that most of us have on some level. Will our husbands' friends be pursuing our sons as they go through their adolescent years? I worried about it. Is it a rational fear? I don't know, but it doesn't stop me from feeling that way.

Q. Now that I know that my husband is gay, do I have to be worried that I have AIDS?

A. I think this is the first thing that comes to the minds of women once the words of "gay" are spoken. They are petrified that they might be infected with AIDS. Obviously, there are still a lot of misconceptions about AIDS or else they wouldn't be so worried. Ironically, most of the women who write to me about this fear haven't had sexual relations with their husbands for years. They have nothing to worry about. Is it possible to get AIDS without sex? Well, I won't say no but the chances of it happening are so remote. AIDS is not airborne, nor can you get it from drinking from the same glass, using the same towel, or sharing the same bed. It is transmitted through blood or semen, so if you and your gay mate have been sharing needles it is possible. Once blood reaches the air, the virus dies within a matter of seconds. So unless your husband has been bleeding on you after he is cut and you have an open wound, I wouldn't worry about it. I tell women that if it will give you peace of mind to be tested, than do it. But there is no reason to have this irrational fear if you haven't had sexual relations with your husband for several years.

But, if your husband has had recent sexual relations with you, then definitely get tested. Even if he tells you that he hasn't acted on his homosexuality, get tested anyway. Gay men coming out to their wives often lie about their sexual experiences because it is too difficult to tell the truth. Sometimes the truth comes out weeks, months, or years later. Sometimes it never comes out. So you do need to protect yourself and get tested.

Even if you haven't had recent sexual relations with your husband in a while, it is good to check out all sexually transmitted diseases—not just AIDS. Numerous women have had complications because they had STDs and were not aware of it until complications prevailed. STDs can fester for a while before they appear so you may think you're safe when you're not.

Letters That Express It All

Each week, I receive an average of 50 – 100 letters from women in pain. These women are from all over the country and the world. To me, they are all different, and yet they are all the same. The circumstances of each woman as far as location, years in the marriage, children, religion, nationality, and occupation are different, but the emotional feelings of despair are all the same.

I send my past newsletters and book chapters everyone who writes to me for help. I try to respond to everyone within a few hours because I know how hopeless this pain makes all of us feel. I have selected a few of these letters to share with you so that you can relate to the despair of others and realize that you are not alone. Some of these letters also express hope for the future—hope that all of us can benefit from. They show us that life can and does move on as long as you are able to let go.

Dear Bonnie,
I just wanted to say thank you. You don't know me from Adam and yet you talked with me as if we were friends. At this time when I question my life and why I am here, it is so nice to know that I have someone like you to talk with. There was a time that I was so depressed that I didn't want to leave the house not even for the day. Now I can, so I know that I will get better.

Part of my response to another letter:
Life will get better if you understand that it is not a life sentence, and you don't have to wait to die to be free.

Dear Bonnie,
I'd like for you to know what a powerful impact this part of your email had on me. I've never put it into words--"I don't have to wait to die to be free." Those words have never come off of my tongue but it is what I felt in my heart. I really did believe that I would just go through life faking happiness until the day I would die and then and only then would I be free of the pain of my loss. I also believe that all things happen for a reason, but I just haven't been able to see it yet. Thank you for your words of wisdom and speaking from the voice of experience.

Dear Bonnie,
I just want to thank you so much for the work that you are doing in this area. It takes tremendous courage to face and use the wounds of your past--and perhaps face them again and again-- each time you work with wives and husbands who seek your help. God bless you and may you continually be given the strength and wisdom to keep giving of your heart in this difficult area.

The pain of many years came to a close when I reached your website and saw the words, "You are not responsible for your husband's homosexuality." I wept through the rest of your site, experiencing the most incredible relief, that other women have had the same struggles, and have emerged more whole. I wanted to embrace my computer monitor and let your words seep into my soul.

I am twenty-six and have been in a relationship with a bisexual man for nine years. We were on the verge of getting married when the truth hit me--that problem I couldn't exactly put my finger on, but which I knew was always there. Once I accepted the real score, many problems just fell into place and made sense. I ended the relationship, and now I feel a very middle-aged twenty-six. I am trying my best to be happy again, trying to hope that perhaps one day, I will be able to invest my heart again, this time, without fear. Thank you so much for your work. Your efforts are not in vain.

Hi Bonnie,
I cry as I write this message. My husband left me 18 months ago for a man. Up until this point I have had no one to talk to about the feelings I had of guilt and rejection. When I read your letter about your feelings, I realized I was no longer alone. Presently we are working through a financial settlement. Since we have two boys, I wish this to be settled quickly, but my ex-husband seems hell bent on trying to destroy me financially as well as emotionally.

I can't understand why he is doing this to me. It's as if he blames me for the 13 years we spent together. I feel cheated. I worked hard to keep our marriage alive, and the hardest thing for me is being a single parent. If I thought or knew that at some point he would leave me for another person, I would never have had children because I didn't want to be a single parent.

Up until Christmas, we had a good friendship developing, but now he can't speak to me without throwing insults. I sometimes feel that this experience has left me so emotionally scarred that I will never be able to trust anyone again. Sorry to go on, but it's just nice to explain my feelings to someone who understands.

Dear Bonnie,
Thank you so much for the articles you sent me. I felt like I was reading my life story for the first time. I have read all sorts of divorce recovery books and information on grieving, and I have been to therapy for a year. (The therapist finally agreed that the pile of evidence I presented was more than just the crazed raving of a scorned woman.) However nothing really addressed the real issue until I "met" you. I always felt like I was out in left field somewhere all by myself with these bizarre issues. I still don't know what to do about my daughters, but I will join your

chat group and maybe some other women can help me decide what to do.

Dear Bonnie,
I read your web site, and I'd like to thank you. Three months ago my husband of 16 years came out. My feelings were pretty much reflected in your anniversary letter. I, too, for many years was led to believe that it was my fault. I knew after I lost 40 pounds, he was out of taunts and complaints about me. Everything from my weight to my religion, my ethic back ground, and to just being a woman was a complaint of his about me. No sooner did I "fix" one thing, he'd find another. Well, I guess you know the drill.

The problem is he doesn't work due to a "chemical imbalance," and he is not yet on disability. His monuMENTAL health bills and insurance are on me. I can't kick a person when he is down, but it seems to me there needs to be an end point. He is home all day long in gay chat rooms, and without a doubt, I am sure he gets "hooked up." Whether gay or straight, whether we are sleeping together or not, I still perceive this as cheating. He states he will be out as soon as disability comes through, but it has been a living hell. This unfairness of it all just blows (pardon the expression) me away.

I feel old, ugly, and undesirable at 46. I would have done a lot better at 30 if he didn't insist on marrying me. Thank you for taking the time to read this.

Dear Bonnie,
Thank you for your recent newsletter. I just have to comment because I could not agree with you more about the "prognosis" about the so called marriages many of us find ourselves in.

I wish I had stumbled on someone to say these things 15 years ago. I would also like to address women who say, "Well,

101

my husband is bad or not very affectionate, or whatever, but really, so far he isn't as bad as or acting out like the others I read about." I went through that, as well, and it's very much like the wife of an alcoholic--we end up the enablers, hoping against hope that we're not really seeing what we're seeing!

I've been married for 21 years with four teenagers, and I do not consider myself to be a "married lady." I am in a no man's land (no pun intended) until I can figure out what to do and how to do it, but there is something freeing in finally calling a spade a spade and detaching from the unrealistic daydream that things will somehow work themselves out. ("The truth will set you free!")

Growing up, my parents seemed to teach us that suffering = piety. When things started to come to light about my husband, I assumed that God was giving me some sort of opportunity to show how stoic and faithful and hopeful I was. I assumed He would rescue me, possibly even throw a small parade in my honor for how trusting I was. These days, I doubt the parade is coming, and I fear I've thrown half of my life away. Pretty sad. On a brighter note, well, I can't really think of one right now, but I DO appreciate your not being wishy-washy or ambiguous in your assessing these situations. You are completely and unfortunately correct, and I am so glad to see someone brave enough to tell the truth...thank you again.

Dear Bonnie,
Two days ago, I found gay sites on our computer that my husband of 36 years had been viewing. I confronted him last night, and he told me that he has had these feelings most of his life. I asked him why he married me, and he said because he loved me! My next question was why he had stayed with me if he has these feelings. His answer was that he could have gotten out at any time, but he loved me and his life and didn't want to leave. I told him that I thought he should leave for his

own happiness. He wants to stay and try to make our marriage work.

As I look back through our past 20 years, I can see all the signs and understand why I never truly felt loved. He is a very caring and wonderful person. He is a great father and has always supported me in all that I have done. I love him dearly and don't want to lose him, but I want him to be happy. I have told him this and he still insists that he loves me and wants to stay with me. He assures me that he has never had a relationship with anyone and never would. He says that he has been for counseling as he has felt guilty all these years for not telling me. WE have two grown children.....our son (married with a year-old daughter) has had a problem with drugs, our daughter's husband left her two years ago for her best friend, and we are living temporarily with my 83 year-old mother who is in congestive heart failure. For me, this is just another crisis that I will weather and live through.

My husband has been self-employed for about 32 years, and we have never had to go without. I wonder if he is worried about what people will think of him. I have assured him that if he wants to leave, we can make up a story that all will believe. He doesn't want our children to know, and I will honor his wishes on that subject. At the present my mind is very clouded, and I can't think very straight. He wants to continue counseling and wants to make our marriage work. I have told him that this decision has to be for his best interest.....he needs to be happy. To be very honest, it will kill me if he leaves me, but I would never tell him that.

What do I do? Am I doing the right thing in supporting him? I don't hate him---I feel so sorry for him as he says his life has been hell. He doesn't want to be this way. Thanks for listening

The Women of the Room

In the fall of 2000, after my book was available, I decided to start an on-line support group to help people through this hardship. I received many requests for referrals to support groups, but not being involved with any, it was impossible for me to recommend any. The former AOL Str8 Spouse support group run by Jean and Dina was the only one I felt comfortable enough to recommend because I believed in the philosophy of the women running the group. They offered an outlet for AOL members, but women with other Internet service couldn't access their support group. I also knew that when you are living this experience, there can never be enough support available.

Since the chatroom began in October or 2000, I have met some of the most wonderful women that anyone could hope to find. They joined my chat after writing to me initially and asking for support. I have had the good fortune to meet several of them in person and plan to meet more of them in the upcoming year.

Although many women passed through the on-line support sessions, this group of women stayed with me consistently, giving hope and guidance to new women who feel isolated and alone. Where other groups have "Pen Pals," I have named this group of women "Pain Pals," because they are very available to alleviate the suffering of others. They do it in our group sessions or one-on-one as I refer other women to them.

We have formed a bond that is stronger than our pain. This bond helps us cope through the day-to-day pressures that we face as wives and ex-wives of gay men. We share our fears, our revelations, our hopes, our dreams, and our hearts. Each of these women is very precious and special to me. No matter how much they think I have given them, they have given me just as much in return. They help restore my energy that often gets zapped after hearing so many unhappy stories that don't seem to have any happy ending in sight.

These are women of strength. They are survivors. They have faced their demons and they are dealing with them. Some of them may be temporarily stuck physically in their marriages, but none of them are imprisoned mentally. They know the truth about their husbands, even if some of their husbands refuse to be honest. They know they are in a transitional phase and eventually they will be totally free of this mismarriage.

These are women that straight men would be blessed to have as wives because they try harder to please than any group of women that I know. That's how they were during their marriages; that's how they are after their marriages for those who are no longer married.

I asked each of them the same set of questions so that you would see how different women in different parts of the country—and world—feel about living through this situation. I think their stories will give you hope and inspiration.

First, let me give you some information about each of these wonderful women.

CHERI

Cheri is 46 years old and lives in Pennsylvania where she works as a court clerk. She was married for 25 years and has two adult children, a daughter and a son. Cheri is the only member of the group that knew her husband was gay prior to marriage. But as a teenager, she believed that once her husband committed to the marriage, homosexuality would not be an issue. When it became an issue twelve years later, they separated for six months. Her husband returned stating that the marriage was more important than his sexual issues. Twelve more years went by and then her husband decided he needed to live his life as a gay man. The two are now separated but remain close friends.

GRETCHEN

Gretchen, age 46, is the mother of two young children, ages six and seven. She lives in Colorado. She was married for 8 years and just recently her husband came to terms with his homosexuality. The couple split up this year. Gretchen is a technical writer and trainer. She is currently the IT Manager at a law firm.

CAROL

Carol, age 47, is the mother of two adult daughters. She lives in Rhode Island. She was married to her husband for 25 years after knowing him for a number of years through school where they were high school sweethearts. After he moved out under the premise of financial problems, she went for counseling where her therapist suggested that homosexuality could be the issue. When she confronted him, he admitted to being "Bi." He now leads an openly gay life. Carol is a legal transcriptionist.

MICHELE

Michelle, age 42, is divorced from her husband. She found out about him last year and the couple split several months later. She has one son, 8 years old. Michele lives in Australia where she works as an aide in a school for special education children. She also owns a pottery business. She remains close friends with her husband.

SYD

Syd, age 60, was the first member of the support chat. She lives in San Rafael, California. She has two grown sons and is also a grandmother. Syd has been married for 35 years but just found out about her husband three years ago. She has recently separated from her husband but is very supportive of him and continues a close friendship.

TAMMY

Tammy, age 38, is married and has two young children. She lives in Georgia where she works as a secretary. Tammy's husband is a practicing homosexual who is in denial due to his deep seeded roots in the Christian community.

KRISTEN

Kristen, age 55, lives in the Seattle, Washington area when she is an administrator for a large health care business. She has been married for nearly 35 years to a man who still refused to be honest with her. Kristen found out about her husband three years ago after finding various gay items in his possession.

BECKY

Becky, age 40, lives in St. Louis, Missouri. She has two young children, a daughter and a son. She has been apart from her husband for five years and divorced for three. Becky is a registered nurse.

---

1. How did you find out about your husband's homosexuality?

Cheri: My husband told me about his being gay when we were still seniors in high school. At 16, I must have led a very sheltered life, because I had no idea what he was talking about, and he had to explain it to me.

Gretchen: My husband totally repressed his homosexual feelings during our life together which I now know was the cause for his behavior towards me and the demise of our marriage. During the difficult time I had reaching the decision to leave him, a good friend counseled me and suggested that my husband might be in denial about his sexuality. The more I thought about it, the more convinced I became this was true. I sought information on the Internet and came across Bonnie's website. Her articles were an uncanny description of life with my husband. I confronted him immediately and he did not deny it. Since then, he has been gradually accepting it and acting upon it.

Carol: After a few months of counseling, I probably always knew it, but put it way back in my mind, but the therapist suggested I ask, so, I did. He said he was bisexual, not a great answer, but anyway, he's never had a girlfriend since, so I guess that makes him GAY.

Michele: Three days after we got home from holidays, he told me that he had met someone else and that the someone else was a 20-year-old guy.

Syd: I had suspected it for about two years, perhaps longer, but finally realized that he was. When he came to me, two days before we were to take a trip to Italy and Greece, he said, "I have something to tell you." I said, "I know, you're gay." He said, "Would you please let ME tell you!" That's the kind of relationship we have.

Tammy: I started suspecting. My first big clue was NO sex. My husband was not interested in me sexually. Even when we did have sex, it was very mechanical, always lacking passion, the passion that comes very naturally between a straight man and a straight woman. Then I started finding evidence of gay porn, men's names and telephone numbers, and eventually I found condoms which obviously were not meant for me. That was when I realized I was dealing with something very real ... much more than looking at pornography ... my husband actually "WAS" gay. I now know that he IS GAY and not bi-sexual. I believe you are either straight or gay, there is no in between. I also believe that being gay is not a choice, it is who you are.

Kristen: I found out about my husband's homosexuality after making some "discoveries." These discoveries included provocative G-string men's underwear, lubricant, condoms, a "butt plug," porn literature and adver-tisements, gay magazines, a huge number of porn videos showing men with men, and the discovery of my husband having a post office box where I believe the majority of these items are received.

Becky: I found out by reading some thoughts he had written down, after returning from a professional meeting out of town. His anger and verbal insults had been increasing since his return. He had changed some habits and become distant. The things I had read talked of lifestyle changes, moving, unknown positives and negatives. I confronted him about 5 days later, after lots of arguing and sleepless nights. He told me of the person he met while out of town. He had looked up locations of gay bars before he left for the conference.

2. Did you have any idea prior to the time of your marriage?

Cheri: Yes.

Gretchen: In retrospect, I always saw things about him, personality quirks, effeminate behavior that scream out

"GAY!" but during our courtship and marriage, I didn't dwell on it. I didn't want to see it. How could he possibly be a gay man if he wanted to marry a woman?

Carol: NO, but looking back now, most of the people he was friends with are gay too.

Michele: I had absolutely no idea until the day he told me and even then I thought maybe that he was lying and it really was another woman.

Syd: NO.

Tammy: I did have some idea even though I was very naïve and ignorant when it came to homosexuality. Someone very close to me shared with me something they knew to be true about my husband. We were very close to our wedding date and I did go straight to him and ask about what I had been told. He quickly assured me that he wasn't gay. Some people had thought that about him simply because he had some gay friends. He assured me that he loved me, wanted to marry me, and that was all I needed to hear. Even if he had been interested in men at any time in the past, he was "over" that and wanted to marry me. Why would a gay man want to get married? Well, needless to say, I had a lot to learn and it has taken me almost 13 years, but I finally know now that GAY is who and what he is, not something he might have thought he was at one time but got it out of his system.

Kristen: No, I did not. If I had suspected my husband was gay, I would have not married him. I believe any gay/straight marriage is doomed for failure. My husband being gay was never even a thought that ever crossed my mind prior to our marriage. I will admit at the time I married my husband, he knew how to cook and clean house, as well as enjoy doing yard work. He had a younger sister and my husband's mother worked. I admired him for not only taking good care of his sister, but also being responsible in helping his family out. I did not consider a man knowing how to cook, clean house, and do yard work a negative. I knew that we would both be working and to me, that meant sharing these responsibilities was a greater help to us. We both enjoyed entertaining family and friends and took pride in a neat house and yard.

Becky: None what so ever. He always pursued the sexual relationship and had lots of interest in my needs or desires.

3. If you confronted him, did he deny it?

Cheri: I did know about his being gay, but at the age I found out, I did not fully understand all the implications or the consequences that would be involved. I had thought that he would be able to give up that part of his life, but if he wanted to go out, as long as he came home to me, it would be okay. I was only 19 years old at the time and thought it would all work out. I asked him several times if he was seeing someone when I was suspicious, but he always denied it. I found condoms in his wallet and in his gym bag, and when I confronted him about them, I was told they were there just in case he met someone while we were separated, or that he had thought about having sex with a guy he met at work, but never followed through with it. It made me suspicious, but to save the marriage I would let it go, and stuff any feelings I had about the whole thing.

Gretchen: When I made the decision to confront him shortly after I realized he was gay, I wanted to be sure to do my best to elicit an honest reaction from him and not to scare him into silence. What I told him was that I thought he was *unsure* about his sexuality and that it was making his life very difficult. I made it clear that I didn't judge homosexuality negatively, that it's something you can't do anything about. He didn't react much to my statements and neither confirmed nor denied having homosexual feelings, which in my mind was an admission. He did adamantly declare that he had never acted upon his feelings with other men, which I have no reason to disbelieve. Our confrontation is the best thing that could have happened to him, I believe. He is finally able to address these long-suppressed feelings and finally discover who he really is.

Carol: When I finally got the nerve to confront him, he said he was BI, not GAY, but, as I said before, he's never had a girlfriend, so…

Michele: This doesn't apply to my situation.

Syd: He came to me and I told him he was gay! If I had confronted him, before he had accepted it himself, I'm sure he would have denied it. He had to come to terms with it on his own time.

Tammy: He denied it that day when I confronted him about the "rumors" I had heard almost 13 years ago now. That was about eight weeks prior to our marriage and we have never mentioned anything about that since. I am still working on finding the right time to make that confrontation now, although life is so much more complicated at this point in my life. I have two beautiful children who will be drastically affected by any outcome of this unfortunate situation.

Kristen: I did confront him after three long agonizing years of keeping this information to basically myself and away from him. I did not share my knowledge or "my discoveries" with anyone for a very long time. In time, I did share it with a couple of my very closest friends, as well as my mother and brother. Up until I received Bonnie's support, no one really knew what to say or how to handle this kind of information. It was (and sometimes still is) a very lonely and confusing time for me. When I finally got the nerve to confront my husband, I told him that I first thought he might be bi-sexual, but then decided he was gay and not bi-sexual. His only comment was, "you're probably right." That is the closest and the one and only time he ever came close to admitting he is gay. This conversation took place only after I initiated it. He told me he had hoped to go to his grave knowing he was and is gay and said he hoped I would never find out. I found it very interesting that my husband never asked what "discoveries" I made at the time nor did I ever elect to share that information with him.

Becky: No. He did think that he did not know what he wanted in his life and kept going back and forth between wanting to divorce and live a gay lifestyle and wanting to remain married and work on our relationship (monogamous).

4. Are you still married at this time? If yes, what is the emotional impact on your mental health by living with a gay husband? If no, how long has your marriage been over and how is the healing process going?

Cheri: Yes, we are still married, but in the process now of separating, after 24.5 years of marriage. The emotional impact of being married to a gay man is becoming clearer to me now than ever before. As I become more aware of the fact that there is no emotional attachment on his part as far as our relationship goes, I realize what I am lacking and now starting to desire in my own life. Until I started getting support from others, I had no idea I had buried my own needs and desires as deep as I had. I figured that by giving him all the love I could without being physical, that I was satisfying my own need to be loved.

Gretchen: We decided to separate six months ago, but have not been able to carry it out sooner because of our economic situation (he is leaving in a few weeks). Once we made the decision to separate, I felt much better about myself, like a great weight had been lifted from me. Once I confronted him about his homosexuality, he has been less emotional and easier to live with. Now I know there was a reason for his horrible behavior towards me; that our marriage didn't fail just because of me. I can forgive him and move forward with my life.

Carol: My marriage has been over for two years (we were separated for three years before divorce). The healing process has been very difficult! In the beginning, I would go out of my way not to meet people that we knew as a couple, I would make sure I would shop in another town, as not to have to meet anyone we both knew, as I didn't want to answer any questions and not to have to explain anything to anyone.

Michele: No, we are not still married and it is coming up to one year on the February 2 since he told me. We separated on the April 2 and the healing process has been slow. I still haven't been out with anyone else, and don't feel ready yet still. But I find it very lonely, as he was my best friend and a good dad and now he is neither.

Syd: We are still married. March will be 38 years. He lived away from home for a year, and it was OK. However, he is back, due to financial reasons. We both have our separate lives, and both have our lives together for our family. It's a very strange arrangement, but one that works for us. We are best friends. The most important thing through the whole process of healing was humor. I was not angry with him when he told me, since I had been angry for too many years due to infrequent sex. I had to come to terms, and am still doing so, that I probably won't be spending the rest of my life with him. This is and was the hardest thing to come to terms with.

Tammy: I am still married and have not made a confrontation yet. I confirmed my suspicions about a year ago and am so glad that I didn't just jump to a confrontation at that time. I know that if I had, he could have made me believe anything he wanted to, just like 13 years ago. Since February of last year, I have made an effort to educate myself. I wanted to learn everything I could about the homosexual lifestyle as well as gather as much concrete information to prove my husband's sexual orientation.

The emotional impact has been profound. In some ways, I feel like a totally different person than who I really am. These men find ways to manipulate, control, degrade and belittle you. They are so self -centered and get so caught up in their little "façade." They lose sight of simple human kindness and consideration. If I had to describe the "gay husband" in two words, it would be SELFISH MANIPULATOR. I realized that he had changed me ... and I did not like who I was becoming.

I came to the point in my life that I was suspicious enough to feel that my husband was gay, but had made the decision that I would stay in the marriage no matter what until my children were older. I would simply exist (I use this word because that's all you do, you can't live – you simply exist and function – to manage the everyday tasks involved in raising a family) in my marriage, accepting the fact that I could not and would not be happy, and that was OK because I owed that to my children. I felt that I had made the conscious decision to become part of this marriage but felt that my children were totally innocent and therefore victims of this straight wife/gay husband *"so-called"* marriage. Technically, I am married, but believe me, a straight woman/gay man marriage is anything but a healthy, nurturing environment in which to live and raise children. If not for my children, I could have walked out the door long ago and never even looked back. The well being, happiness and stability of my children are one of my greatest concerns.

Then, I met a wonderful straight man. Someone I became very close to. He was someone who I could talk to and someone who truly listened to me and cared about me. As our relationship grew, I had feelings that I had not felt for years. He made me want to be happy again. He helped me to see that I could and did deserve to be happy. He is the very first person that I was able to actually say the words "MY HUSBAND IS GAY" to. I remember how scared I was the day I wrote those words, I was so afraid that would change our relationship and the way he felt about me ... forever. But, I felt that this was such a major part of my life and it was very unfair to keep this from him anymore, and he made me feel comfortable enough and trust him enough that I could tell him anything. His reaction was total love and support and understanding, which was what I needed. That showed me that the people who truly loved and cared about me would not judge ME for what my husband did ... and the others, it really doesn't matter anyway. THAT was the beginning of me being able to accept and start to deal with my situation.

Then, I found Bonnie's website. After reading Bonnie's first book, working with Bonnie and our wonderful support group, I have come to realize that none of this is my fault, there is absolutely nothing I could do that would change this and that I deserve and can be happy. That is what I am working on at this point ... a normal, healthy life for my children and me.

Kristen: Yes, I have been married for almost 35 years. The emotional impact on my mental health in living with a gay husband carries a tremendous weight and knowing I've made that choice for now continues, at times, to be extremely difficult. My husband refuses to acknowledge he is gay and wants to act straight and pretend we live a normal married life like our other friends and to everyone else we meet and know. There is never a day that goes by when I'm not reminded that we're both pretending that everything is okay when in fact, it's really not. Not being true to myself has been extremely difficult. I feel like I am living a lie and am not facing the true realities of this whole situation. I feel the times that are most difficult is when he is emotionally and verbally abusive and I am not willing or strong enough at times to stick up for myself. I find I go to bed later than my husband and I find I have continued to find ways of "detaching myself" from my husband. I go to things on my own or with other friends who are "my" friends. Over the years, I have supported my husband in going to his office functions and meeting business associates from his office. My husband has always made me feel like his business associates are more important than mine and he is very selective in what office functions of mine he attends. My spouse has always made me feel like my management position is not as important or as lucrative as his. What an understatement...perhaps earning five times more than me has something to do with it. Today, I tend to have work associates and friends with simpler tastes in life that are more concerned with helping other and earning less money. Some of my closest friends struggle to survive and have made choices in their careers to do things for others that make them happy rather than maximize their earnings at this point in life. In other words, our mutual friends are friends who are far more materialistic in life. Don't get me wrong. I enjoy the good life as much as anyone else; however, I admire those who have chosen other paths along the way and who give something back to their communities and others and who consciously try to live their lives as better people and who are more concerned for others. Our children are now grown and are married. For many years, I felt we just had a lousy marriage and I stayed in it for the sake of our children. Having children made coming home from work all seem so worthwhile. Now that our children are grown and are young adults and are away from home, it's just my husband and me. I feel like I've been left with a hard shell at times and all that kept this shell alive and vibrant is now gone. Sometimes it's hard for me to leave work at night knowing that my husband is at home. I look forward to him traveling in his work. This gives me the peace and freedom I long for in my life.

Becky: I have been divorced for almost two years. The healing process has gone up and down. It has been four and a half years since he moved out of the house and at times I think like I should be at a place further down the road than I am. Sometimes I don't think I know how to stop loving a person you have spent so much time with and shared so much with. Separating the emotional and intellectual side of this process has been difficult. My healing position also is reflected on how my children are doing at the time. If they are being affected in a negative way by the actions of their father than I tend to sink back to that angry phase. Then at times I find myself having a great deal of pity for him. I know him well enough to understand some of the reasons for his actions or lack of

118

them even if it isn't what he is saying or doing at the time. I feel sorry for him because I know he doesn't like who he is, but he can't have everything he wants or thinks he wants. I move on with my life because I know I have to and I put on a good face at times. I need to move forward because my kids need me to.

5. What issues have been the most difficult for you? (I mean issues such as isolation, self-esteem, trust, etc.)

Cheri: Trust. I can honestly say that I lost all trust in him when I walked in and found him with another man in our home. After that night, I did forgive him, but I have never forgotten the feelings that took over my whole being in those first few minutes. On several other occasions I found condoms, and was told they were either old, or he had been thinking of being intimate with someone, but never went through with it. I always had doubts in the back of my mind. My self esteem level was never that good to begin with, so when we decided to get married, I guess in a way I settled without realizing, thinking that it may be the only chance at marriage I had. I did and do honestly love him very much, and he does love me as much as he is capable of, but I know now that it is not enough.

Gretchen: I distinctly remember the day after I made the realization what his problem was. I felt like someone had punched me in the stomach. I was very down on myself; "How could you be so stupid! How could you be so desperate that you had to marry a fag?! Aren't you going to look like a fool when everyone finds out!" A good long cry and many hours on the phone with a friend got that out of my system. I am a bit chagrined that everyone who knows us both has known right away that my husband is gay, but everyone has been sympathetic which has helped tremendously. I can honestly say my self-esteem has improved greatly because I am no longer being subjected to constant criticism and negativity. I let him drag me down quite a bit during our marriage and am very proud to say that as he exits my life, I am regaining my identity as a worthwhile, intelligent, beautiful woman!

Carol: After the separation I was very isolated, not wanting to talk to anyone that we both knew, staying away from places where we both went. Actually, the first few months, I had problems even looking at people (kissing, holding hands, I even had problems buying greeting cards). I would have a problem seeing such things as Valentine's Day cards or Christmas cards etc. Self-esteem, I had NONE and as for trust, I can't say that even now, I have much trust in anyone! It takes me a long time to trust anyone new.

Michele: All those issues you list are difficult. They all seem to fit. It is very hard. I have had people say that maybe I focus too much on the gay side of it, but that is everything to do with Mark now. He is truly like another person now; he just hasn't changed sleeping partners, his whole way of life has changed. He is gay and their lives are way different. Trust will be a hard one as I lived with Mark for ten years and I find now that it wasn't who he was. And I had absolutely no idea. But with me it wasn't the physical betrayal, it was the emotional betrayal. So it will be hard to trust again, but I am sure that I will meet someone in the future whom I will trust, when I am ready.

Syd: My self-esteem was not affected when I found out. I think it was low for many years prior. I do not blame myself, nor am I angry with him for being gay. I understand. The biggest issue I have is that we probably won't grow old together. Not to make light about it but, if I had a penis, everything would be perfect! That's just the way it is. I didn't cause him to be gay.

Tammy: I deal with several issues that are very difficult for me. I think trust is the big one. When you realize that you are married to a gay man, suddenly, everything you have done in for the time you have been married has been a lie. Nothing is genuine and you feel that you have just LOST that part of your life. For me, it has been 13 years. I can honestly say the only positive, good thing that has come out of my 13-year marriage is my two beautiful children. Other than that, everything is so useless. I feel that I lost 13 of the best years of my life.

Another thing I deal with is fear. I am afraid of so many things. I worry about being embarrassed if this comes out. I worry about what other people will think about my children and me. I worry about finances when I finally make my confrontation and my husband and I divorce. I worry most about my children and the impact this will have on them.

Kristen: Oh, gosh…where do I start?

Self-esteem – Somewhere along the way, I've forgotten to take care of myself. I have gained a lot of weight and need to take charge of me. I know I need to exercise regularly and lose a good 75 to 80 pounds. I need to make this a priority. Although I've never been thin, I've totally lost control. Sadly, I bought a book once entitled. "When Food Is Love." That's really disgusting, isn't it? I love to cook and eat out either at lunch or dinner. I realize I can still do this; however, I need to make better choices whenever I do. One other thing that I have dealt with is that my husband buys a new car every two or three years. Many years ago, I got the cars he previously drove and now he trades them in. He expects me to look on the "Used Car lot" whenever I need a car. Today, I drive a car that is 11 years old while he drives a brand new car. Tonight, on Valentine's Day, as we were out to dinner with friends, he told me that if I could afford a new car, I could get whatever car I could pay for. In other words, in his mind, his executive salary allows him to have new cars---my salary doesn't. What signal does that send? It's very degrading and makes me feel like "I'm not worthy of ever having a new car in my life." He uses the words, my boat, my house, my car, my son... Perhaps I'm overly sensitive at this point, but I can't help notice how saying things like this really hurts. I believe I'm at a point in my life that no matter what is said or done, I'm going to feel hurt, left out, cheated, verbally and emotionally abused, etc.

Holidays – Holidays continue to be challenge. We celebrate all holidays with my mother and her companion and our children. It is a stressful time as we continue to pretend that all is well and we're family. My husband plans our holiday menus with our daughter and then tells me what we're going to have. Valentine's Day is the absolute worst holiday of all to tolerate. All the advertising and constant reminders make it unbearable at times. The sadness I feel is due to lost hopes and dreams and the crossroads I find myself in at this stage in my life. I feel cheated that I'm now middle age and am facing what I'm facing. While I am married, I feel very much alone. Knowing my husband refuses to admit he's gay only makes it worse. To me, this represents total selfishness and he totally disregards the affects on my life. I miss having someone to love, talk to, laugh with, touch, and cherish in my life. At times, I feel very much alone even though I'm married and am currently still with my spouse.

Isolation – Being the only one in our circle of friends married to someone gay is a very lonely and isolated feeling. Although I realize there are many gay/straight marriages out there that exist, I feel I'm the only one among our friends and the other people we know. Because my husband has chosen to not come out, I too, have not come out. Although I've told my brother and mother, they really don't know how to react. My mother expects things to get better and she just wants this to be a bad dream and all go away. She's older and this information is just "too big" for her to handle in life. She loves my husband, and yet gets frustrated when she sees him being disrespectful to me. She doesn't want to stir up the pot, so she listens to him and then tells me later how she could never stand being around someone like that in her own life. My dear mother stated at one time that she and my father didn't always see eye to eye on everything. She's comparing disagreeing to living in a gay/straight marriage. I see this as comparing apples and oranges. My one and only brother remains detached as he normally has in life with all family situations. Being my husband is in denial, my husband and I do not openly talk about him being gay and consequently do not share this with each other. Once again, he's gay, but wants to "act straight" and go to his grave without anyone ever knowing. Too bad, I blew that for him by confronting him with this. Our communication is very poor. At night, my husband traditionally reads the newspaper, a book or magazine, and flips TV channels every night. We hardly speak to each other. Although I continue to try to initiate conversations, it's tough. I do not have the emotional support I deserve. Often, I feel as alone with my spouse sitting right next to me as I do when he's out of town.

Lack of support – At one time, I asked my mother if she would lend me the money to pay for the retainer fees for my attorney. Although my mother is financially very comfortable, she hesitated even when I assured her I would make regular payments and could certainly have it paid for within a matter of a few months. My mother also has a new condo (totally paid for) she's never lived in. She lives with a companion in his house. I asked if I could live there (not rent free) until the dust settled with my divorce. Once again, she didn't feel it would work for us to live together even though she doesn't even live in her condo nor has she for over three years. So, in other words, not only do I not have the support of my husband, my family isn't really there for me either. I consider myself always there for them whenever they need me and they know they can count on me to come through.

Trust – I've lost all my trust in my husband. Being we do not openly communicate with each other, I have no idea what's really going on in his life. He won't talk about being gay. At times, I'm sorry I even confronted him. It's gotten me nowhere. I should have just divorced him due to our lousy marriage...period. I had enough stuff going on without even addressing the gay/straight issues that exists. He takes good care of himself by buying a new car every two or three years, buys the best clothes, and basically gets what he wants whenever he wants it. I wish he would just tell me where he's at in his life. Ideally, I'd like him to release me and set me free. I resent being the one who has to make the first move because he doesn't have the guts to do it himself.

Loss of Identity – At times, I question who I really am. I don't feel I truly know the real me anymore. Not having an emotional or physical attachment to your spouse can do some real damage to one's ego. It's been so long since I've made my own decisions about buying furniture, decorating my house the way I want, having a pet in my life, going or not going to the places I want to go or don't want to go, etc., etc. As I look around our house, it represents my husband and his taste. Although he has good taste, he refuses to accept my opinions about how to furnish our home if he disagrees. He just goes out and buys whatever he wants to buy whenever he wants to buy it. I used to like who I was and now, so many times, I feel disappointed in myself in being so non-confrontational and not sticking up for me. I let other things in life become a higher priority and forget to take care of me. This needs to change quickly!

Bedtime and After Work Habits – To avoid going to bed with my husband, I stay up much later than I should and consequently get very tired. When I get up some mornings, I feel like I've been hit with a "Mac" truck. As mentioned before, I also stay at work late quite often in order to avoid going home. Some of my best times are when he's out of town.

Disapproving Looks/Nagging – My husband has a knack for giving me looks of disapproval. At times, he doesn't say what he's thinking, but his looks say it all. I'm trying not to let him get away with it and when I see him doing this, I ask him what he's thinking or whatever. He reminds me when my lipstick has worn off. He can't see why on weekends, I might not want to put on makeup when I'm around the house cleaning on weekends. He feels the need to comment about everything and does it in a very offensive manner.

Discoveries – Since making the discoveries I made some time ago, I have found a "magnetic force" that draws me into monitoring what things are there and where he's hidden them. Although I've gotten much better about this, I find I sometimes slip back, and then look to see what new DVDs, VHS movies, magazines, or whatever is there. In the beginning, I even briefly watched some of "his" movies to confirm what I already knew. How sick is this? In the very beginning of my discoveries, I felt I needed to confirm my suspicions. Now, it makes me wonder why I continue to do this? It gets me nowhere and only makes me feel much worse.

Financial Concerns – This is a big issue for me. I am now a baby boomer and should be comfortable in my life.

Our kids are grown and on there own, but I don't have a clue where my husband and I stand financially. This truly scares me. At this stage in my life, I want some security in knowing that my life will not be a total financial disaster when our marriage dissolves. I guess that's something for the attorneys to decide. There is something to be said for the peace of mind one gets when they no longer are faced in dealing with a gay "pretend to be straight" marriage.

Family & Friends – I need to let this play out and not worry about how everyone will react when my husband and I divorce. I know things will never be the same and hopefully this change will benefit everyone down the road. I don't really think our friends will be as surprised about the change in our lives. Hopefully, they'll be happy that we've (I've) finally decided to move on.

Religion – At one time, this was more of an issue. The marriage vows…til death due us part…Well, I have to believe that God doesn't want me to be celibate for the rest of my life and be married to a gay man. Although I hate being a divorce statistic in life, I need to get a life before it's too late. Time is passing and I'm not getting any younger.

Physical & Mental Well Being – I spoke earlier on about the emotional impact. This truly has taken a toll on me physically and mentally, as well. As mentioned, I'm overweight and need to get regular exercise. I'm currently on high blood pressure medication, too. Although the above two conditions are directly connected, I have to believe that being in my marriage doesn't help any of the above conditions. My husband constantly reminds me of, "How fat do you want to be?" and "Do you ever think you'll ever do something about it?" He then proceeds to eat a bag of microwave popcorn or polish off a Ben & Jerry's ice cream carton right in front of me and then tells me he needs to lose some weight, too. He also pokes me in the stomach (which I hate and I've told him to stop it) or puts his hand under my chin as a reminder to do something about my excess weight in both these areas. I would hope to someday meet someone who I can share my life. If it happens...it happens. If not, so be it. Once again, I need to get some of this excess weight off.

Becky: How to even begin this?? Isolation.....YEAH! At times I try to tell myself it is no different than any other divorce where the husband has had an affair. I really didn't know how to explain exactly what I felt. Only my ex's family and a few local friends really know the reason for my divorce. Self-esteem......it didn't take much to crush what I have or had. I put on a good front and I am working at making myself a priority. I do understand that if I don't look out for my own needs no one is going to do it for me. Trust.....I don't trust anything my ex -husband says or does. I find myself more pessimistic than I used to be about people or life. I haven't had a relationship with another man, post tgo, so I don't know how I will react to another intimate relationship. I think I fear that because trust is very important to me. I don't like to not feel like I can trust people in my life.

6. What can you share about your sex life? When you met your husband, did you have much previous sexual experience?

Cheri: I had very little sexual experience before my husband, and now realize that I never had a satisfying relationship with anyone I had dated before him. We did have sex often in the beginning, sometimes very satisfying, other times only for his satisfaction. He drank a lot and I now think the reason for this was so that he could get through those moments of intimacy. He was not always drinking before sex, but more times than not. Once he began going to AA, our sex life dwindled until it stopped all together, 11 years before the end of our marriage. Also, I was sexually abused by an uncle when I was 11 yrs old, and I somehow think that this caused a lot of the conflicts I had about sex itself. He did like to cuddle, and still does go to sleep with his arms around me. After sex, he liked to stay close for a while, which I am realizing is not common. But I found it comforting, and I guess in his own way, he did too.

Gretchen: We met in graduate school. I am seven years older than he is. I did have a lot of experience with men before I had met him; he had only slept with one woman. At first, I found his lack of experience somehow endearing. He didn't try to get me into bed on the first date like so many others. When he did finally try to have sex with me, he couldn't get an erection for several tries. Although I knew men who were better lovers, I found he had other qualities that at the time were more important. During our marriage, we seldom had sex and it was never satisfying for me (always "man-on-top-get-it-over-with quick!"). I came to repress my urges in order not to be rebuffed and disappointed. He always blamed my weight on his not being attracted to me. Even during times I lost weight, he never found me attractive enough. At least now, I know the real reason.

Carol: Absolutely none! Five years separated, two years divorced, still none, and not looking for anyone!

Michele: My previous knowledge of sex before I met Mark was good. I had always had a good healthy sex life. I met Mark when I was 33 and had my son when I was 34 (my first child) and our sex life was good until about four years ago. And at the same time Mark came down with a nerve syndrome and all his nerve endings were enlarged and I put our non-existent sex life down to that. I didn't want to put pressure on him and he seemed okay with it, so I thought this was just how it would be from now on.

Syd: I was pretty naïve. As I look back on our married life, sex was not great. It was infrequent, and I became very frustrated. It was not a big part of our life. I was the one who always took the initiative and reams have been written about that subject.

Tammy: Our sex life has been basically non-existent compared to a straight man/woman relationship. We have had no sex since my daughter was conceived almost five years ago now. Even when we did have sex, it was very mechanical; at times it was difficult, if not impossible. I was almost always the one to initiate sex. Then as time went on, my husband did feel guilty (I think) and began to come up with a million different reasons why he could not perform. At that point, I thought it was my problem. For whatever reason, I wasn't what I should or needed to be to make him desire me or to satisfy him. Well, I now realize that I could NOT satisfy him, I simply didn't have what it takes BUT it wasn't my fault. I can never make my husband happy because I'm not a man.

I did have sexual experience prior to marriage. I was involved in a five-year relationship with a very straight, thoughtful, caring guy. We had a very normal, passionate, active sex life. Having this previous experience was one of the most important clues I had. I KNEW that even when my husband and I did have sex, it just wasn't right, wasn't what it should be. Something was always missing … the passion.

Kristen: My sex life…it no longer exists and I have none. Unlike some women, I do very much miss having a sexual relationship. I have now resorted to "toys" to help relieve some of my needs; however, I miss the touching, holding, caressing, tender kisses, and falling asleep in someone else's arms not to mention pure sex with a straight male. My husband and I last had sex six years ago and neither of us even talked about why that happened. I have certainly figured it out by now, but it took me three years of wondering why and what went wrong along the way. Before I met my husband, I lived in an era where having sex before marriage was taboo. I did play around and got close to "going all the way" before marriage, but never did. My mother was successful in putting the fear of God in me saying that I might get pregnant if I ever had sex before marriage. I would say my previous sexual experiences were limited to hugging, kissing, and heavy petting prior to getting married.

7. Do your children know? How are they reacting?

Cheri: Our daughter is almost 24 years old. She called home from college three years ago, and asked me how I would feel if she were to tell me she was a lesbian. I told her that I would love her all the same, and that if she felt she was, to be honest with herself. I just wanted her to be happy. It was at this time that my husband and I decided to tell her about his being gay. At this time she seemed to accept it okay. Now that we are separating, it appears she has more issues with it, and is having a hard time dealing with her father in a lot of ways. She feels now that he is shoving it down her throat by being more open with it. Our son is 22 years old. He is a different story all together. He has never had a close relationship with his father; there was always tension and animosity between them. He feels his father never really tried to be close to him, and that his father always expected perfection from him. We told him this past summer when we decided to separate that his father is gay, and I feel he knew, but never really wanted the confirmation. Since finding out, it seems that he is pulling even farther away from any emotional attachment to his father.

Gretchen: Our children are only 5 and 6 years old; they are far too young to understand this aspect of our divorce. At this point, I have no idea how this subject will be handled in the future, if at all. It will depend on how my husband deals with it himself. I have always told him that it doesn't matter whether he's a homosexual; if he isn't happy with himself and his life, he won't be able to be the best father he can be.

Carol: My children know now. I have two girls, now 26 and 24, but when he left they were 21 and 17. The 21 year old was living in Florida at the time so she was really not around for the mess, but the one 17 was around for everything! He decided he wanted to tell them both. The older one was home for a week for a vacation and he said he was going to tell her, but as the week went by, he never told her. The day before she left, I told her, and, boy, was he mad at me for doing that. He said I "stole his thunder." He didn't speak to me for about a month for that! He finally told the younger daughter about a month later and he said he thought she took it very well; but we, my daughter and I, were living together alone, without any support from him (she was only 17 at the time and he contributed NOTHING towards her support) came home crying hysterically, so, I don't think she took it as well as he thought!

Michele: My son knows. He is eight. He has known from the start. At the moment, he isn't fazed about it. He just loves his dad. It seems to be a bit more accepted over here and kids seem to think that's the way it is sometimes.

Syd: Our boys are grown, with children of their own. The night my husband told the boys was very tough for him. For once in my life, I kept my mouth shut and let him do all the talking. Both are very supportive. One is more understanding than the other. Both learned a great deal about their growing up days, and why they didn't have a real father – a "jock-O."

Tammy: I have not made the confrontation, so obviously, my children do not know. Even when I do make that confrontation, I will not tell my children at this point. They are too young and I think they will eventually figure it out. When they are to that point, I hope that my husband and I have a relationship that permits us to be considerate enough of each other and our children and can sit down together and talk about it.

Kristen: To my knowledge, our children do not know. Truthfully speaking, I consider our children very bright and I suspect they possibly know their father is different than many other fathers they've known over the years. My husband loves to cook, decorate, is a very successful executive and has been a responsible father to our children. He is very meticulous in his appearance and sees that he takes good care of himself. He buys the very best clothes and gets whatever he wants whenever he wants it. I'm sure our children (who are now young adults) have been aware of us not touching, kissing, etc. How could they ever think that we represent a normal husband and wife team? I'm sure they know something is definitely wrong, but I doubt they'll ever bring whatever thoughts they have about our marriage up in conversation.

Becky: When I met my husband I had had several rela-tionships that were sexually intimate. Some long term and some very casual. I had some relationships with boyfriends that were longer term than others. I think there were also times when I had sex without allowing much emotional attachment (even though I didn't always admit it to myself). My ex-husband was usually the initiator of our sexual relationship. He always wanted me to be more spontaneous. He was always concerned about if I had my needs met and if there was anything I wanted him to do differently. He was not shy about expressing affection in public appropriately. We spent lots of time after sex cuddling and would have preferred I not have a nightgown on. He would suggest the showers and baths, light the candles etc. Even after he moved out of the house, he remained very interested and initiated lots of sexual contact. Even a year after the divorce and 3 years after he moved to live with the boyfriend, he expressed an interest in having a sexual encounter!!!!!

8. What advice can you give other women who are just finding out about their husbands or trying to cope in their marriages until they are able to become independent?

Cheri: I think the most important thing that these women need to know is that they are no way in responsible for their husbands' sexual preference. It is also very important to get support form other women who have been going through this to see that they are not alone. I think the feeling of isolation adds to the distress of trying to deal with all the confusing feelings that come from finding out. There are a lot of things that we do not understand about homosexuality, and the confusion only adds to the feeling of helplessness. Hearing others stories and how they have dealt with issues as they came up is essential to beginning the healing process.

Gretchen: It seems to me that when women first find out, they always blame themselves for this turn of events. That somehow, they are at fault or should share in the blame for their marriage failing. I can't imagine something further from the truth. I hope women can take some comfort knowing that there's nothing they could have done, that they will be better off in many ways without their husbands. I also hope they can find a little comfort in knowing they're not alone. I never imagined how many others are going through this until I found this support group.

Carol: Oh, that's probably the hardest question in this whole questionnaire. I would probably say, find a friend, someone you can count on, through thick and thin, who won't judge you or what you're going through. Be strong, be true to yourself and believe in what you can be. Remember what you were and who you were before you met him and keep your chin up, things will get worse before they get better but, when they get better, it will be so much better for you, as a person, than it was with him!

Michele: My advice is if they are still in a marriage to get out. Lies just hurt yourself and your children. It is a hard road but you have to take it someday, so the sooner the better I think. Try to keep things as normal as you can for the kids. It makes it a lot easier on them if things around them stay familiar. It is hard because it seems most times the guys just don't want to be around. I know Mark was a good dad when we were married, and now he is happy to see Ryan two nights, every four weeks. And he has unlimited access. He can come and see him anytime, take him any weekend. But I think children cramp the gay lifestyle a bit, though the men will tell you that they are the best fathers and how hard done by they are.

Syd: DO NOT be hard on yourself! Always remember, it's not your fault, you didn't do anything to cause him to be gay. If you can remember, and believe that, you'll be OK.

Tammy: If you are just finding out about your husband, my advice to you is to take your time, think about what is happening, seek guidance and support from others who truly KNOW what you are going through (Bonnie will be your greatest asset) and last but not least, gather and secure all the information and evidence you need to confirm your suspicions. Once you have a clear head and have an idea what it is that you want and what's best for your children, set goals and make plans for your future. Everybody's timetable and map is going to be different. It is taking me a long time, but I want to make sure I do everything right.

I am still in the "coping in my marriage" stage. I would not recommend staying at this point indefinitely. Sometimes I feel that I have everything under control and am moving in the right direction and then one day, for reasons I don't know and can't explain, I feel like the rug has been pulled right from under my feet and I feel like a total wreck. Those are the days I write to Bonnie and pour my heart out. She reassures me that everything will happen and that I will be OK. Trying to live in this stage is so difficult, living from one day to the next, never knowing what to expect.

Kristen: If your spouse admits he's gay, if possible, try to continue to have an open dialog. Don't be hasty in making any quick life altering decisions. Take some time to sift through your emotions and have a game plan in mind, but don't take forever. Don't let him get away with shutting you out by trying to spare you from being hurt. Only you know how much you can take or how much you want to know. Try to get control over this as soon as possible before it starts causing physical side affects. In this case, I don't believe silence is golden...silence can often hurt a lot more than knowing the truth. I think it's best to seek support with those who you feel can best understand what you're going through. Bonnie has offered the support I truly needed that works and speaks to me. Beware of support groups that do not meet your needs or are not in line with your thinking. Beware of "professionals" to try to tell you to just "stick it out" or tell you "things could be a lot worse." It is sometimes very difficult to find the right professional help at times, too. There are few professionals out there who truly understand the magnitude of what it's really like in finding out you're married to someone who you thought was straight and now you find out your spouse is gay! I think it's very wrong to stay in a marriage and let your husband "get away" with calling all the shots and accepting less than what you deserve in a marriage. I would recommend that if you find out your husband is gay, get out...the sooner the better. It's a dead-end street and does not get better. Seek proper legal counsel. Getting out of the marriage allows you the freedom to potentially lead a more healthy and normal life and perhaps even meet someone who can love and offer the emotional support and the intimacy you deserve. While I did not know my husband was gay until fairly recently, I knew that our marriage was on the rocks for a very long time. I just kept making excuses for so many years and didn't want to face a failed marriage. I spent so many years in trying to figure out what was wrong with me. I have bought so many self-help books and always wanted to improve the person I felt I needed to be in order for our marriage to survive. I got the positive strokes at work and from friends, but got all the negative comments and put downs at home. I hated the idea of being a divorce statistic and couldn't bear what a divorce would mean to our children.

I kept putting off leaving even though things never got better. There were always big occasions to keep me in the marriage. Even after confirming that my husband was gay, I have continued to stay in my marriage due to family events; e.g., graduations, weddings, first grandchildren, etc. You get the picture. Always some excuse...soon the years slip away and one tires of listening to hearing you talk about the same subject. The last point I'd like to make is, if your spouse is gay; don't ever think you'll ever change him to ever be a straight spouse. It's not going to ever happen so don't be fooled. I am lucky in that I've never felt I could (nor would I want to) ever change my spouse to be straight. It's an unnatural progression and you'll end up on the short end of the stick, believe me. Also, I suggest you read and gain more knowledge so that you are prepared to take whatever steps are necessary to get on with your life.

Becky: They do not know about "Dads" sexual orientation. They know "Dad" has a roommate that is a man. Dad lives 1100 miles away and talks on the phone or visits them very inconsistently. They have been to visit Dad twice. Dad sleeps with them while the boyfriend sleeps in another room.

9. In retrospect, were there possible signs that you missed during your marriage before you knew the truth that you can share for other women?

Cheri: N/A

Gretchen: The signs were all over the place, but being the modern, liberal, non-judgmental woman I like to feel I am, I swore up and down that I was imagining things! "Not all effeminate men are gay! Just because he doesn't like to have sex doesn't mean anything! He was probably looking at a lingerie ad when I caught him masturbating to *Men's Health.*" My husband's father turned out to be gay as well, and came out right before he died of AIDS. There is scientific evidence of a genetic link in homosexuality. It's so much easier to see and accept these signs after the truth is known. It's truly something you can avoid looking at closely when you don't want to face it.

Carol: Oh boy, lies, mostly lies. I was very trusting and I have said all the time that I gave him enough rope and HE HUNG ME. I think I was a very trusting person. No matter where he wanted to go or things he wanted to do, I would always say, go, that's a great opportunity. But, looking back, he had many business meetings, business trips, odd phone calls, too many gay friends, and nervous any time I would ask about any of them.

Michele: No.

Syd: Lack of interest in sex.

Tammy: There are numerous things! As they say, "Hindsight is 20/20" ... this is so true. I look back at so many things and think, "I should have known." At the beginning of our marriage, when most couples can't get enough of each other, I always had to initiate sex, and it was so empty. Then I think about the fact that while all our friends were planning and setting goals and dreaming about new houses, new vehicles, better positions in their careers, starting families, my husband never wanted to even talk about those things other than the fact that he was more than eager to have children. I think that was probably his security, knowing that was a major commitment to me, and it would make it more difficult for me to leave should I ever find out.

138

My husband went to bed early every single night, so that he was asleep by the time I came to bed so that he didn't have to feel guilty for not having sex with me. He is always coming up with excuses to not accompany the kids and me to my parents' house, to family functions, etc. He wanted his time at home alone on the computer or phone or whatever. And the pornography -- it was over whelming when I really started to realize what was going on.

If you even have an idea that your husband might be gay, he probably is. If he has given you any reason to wonder, don't let it drop. Stay on it until you satisfy your curiosity and save your sanity. Don't let him get by with telling you that it was only a passing phase, it wasn't what you really thought, others were doing it, but not me. And the biggie -- I am attracted to other men, but I would NEVER act on it. As I have said, I haven't confronted my husband but just from what I have learned, gay men are so promiscuous and I was absolutely stunned at some of the things I found my husband to be involved in and how close he was doing these things to home.

Kristen: Whenever we went on a vacation and we were at a beach, my husband would always want to walk the beach by himself or with my girlfriend's husband. He never asked me to go with him. He also bought a Speedo swimsuit (which surprised the heck out of me) one year and actually wore it on the beach. We were with another couple that are long time friends and they were equally surprised, if not shocked, when they saw my husband. I would consider my husband conservative and one who generally wears "boxer looking" swimsuits. It should have been a bigger clue to me when my husband and I stopped having sex six years ago and neither of us ever talked about why that was. I was afraid to ask. Once again, I blamed myself. I had gained weight and felt that I was to blame. Because I consider myself an optimist, I think I was always too pre-occupied in wanting to fix my marriage and continue to try to make things better. I thought our marriage was not going well and it was because of me and I could not longer find the "right buttons" to push. I never even stopped to think of what I wasn't getting out of our marriage…and look too deep. The thoughts were too painful. So, if this happens, don't hesitate to ask why and don't settle for a flimsy response. It should have also been a clue when my husband wanted to try having sex "doggy style" over the other ways we were used to. While trying something new can often be exciting, we never seemed to be successful in trying something new or having sex in the ways we "normally" did before. He keeps secrets and doesn't let you into financial matters and things that should normally be shared by spouses. My husband has always been very controlling. Early on in our marriage, I liked being taken care of and I lived in a time where husbands took care of their wives and dealt with all the finances, etc. I admired this and felt that this was the way things should be. As I matured and became more independent, I realized that not talking about certain things such as where we stood financially, etc. was very wrong. Whenever I would question certain things, my husband was very manipulative and was successful in making me feel like things were in good hands. I think that if you do not feel you have a spouse who you can openly share things with, there is something is wrong.

Becky: I wish I could identify them if there were. Many people with various different problems share the controlling issues he had.

10. Was your husband emotionally abusive to you?

Cheri: I think looking back now, there were times when he was emotionally abusive. There were things he said to me that have affected the way I feel about myself. He told me, after a six-month separation, that we were no longer going to have sex because the thought of it made his blood run cold and his skin crawl. That made me feel really good! It has always stayed with me and made me wonder about myself. I know now that it was his issue, and had nothing to do with me, but it still comes back to haunt me. Other things he has said, which after I told him how I felt about them, he would say he did not mean them to sound the way they did. He told me the reason he wants to separate is that he is tired of getting a whiplash every time a man walks by and he cannot go after him, and that he wants to be free to pursue a relationship with a man, although there is no one in the picture now, but he does not want to have any doubts later in life. These things added to my low self-esteem and add up to a form of emotional abuse, although in the long run, he is very sensitive to hurting me consciously. I guess we just look at things differently sometimes, and he does have a hard time expressing himself, verbally and emotionally.

Gretchen: YES. I can't believe the years of verbal and sometimes physical abuse I put up with. I have always been 40-50 pounds overweight, and had been subjected to years of nagging and cajoling to lose weight, even after two therapists told my husband how coun-terproductive that behavior was. My husband was hypercritical about many other aspects of our life together as well, to the point where friends and relatives would comment on his disrespect towards me. The physical abuse was occasional and not severe, but two incidents in two months truly got me going to end the marriage. I now recognize a pattern in his abuse. He would go through mood cycles, slowly building up to a confrontation that required many hours of argument about insignificant things, often going back years. Then, once he got it out of his system, he would be a totally loving, affectionate husband until his mood started to give way again. It was an awful way to live, walking on eggshells around him. I realize now that his repression and denial had such a tremendous psychological affect on him. I was the perfect foil; by having someone to criticize and focus on, he could avoid focusing on himself. Since he has now reached a certain degree of acceptance of his sexuality, the confrontation cycles have stopped!

Carol: Absolutely! I would get dressed to go out and thought I looked great (you know when you look really good), and he would say, "Are you going to wear that?" or, "Are you going to wear those shoes, what's with those earrings, why aren't you wearing the bracelet I put out for you?" He would just have so many cynical comments that I just thought I was so dumb or just plain stupid that I couldn't even figure out a wardrobe for myself! He always made be feel like no one would ever want my opinion on ANYTHING because I was so dumb or really incompetent on the subject of life in general.

Michele: No.

Syd: No.

Tammy: I would have to answer yes, reluctantly. He was not verbally abusive to me in an intentional or direct way, but emotionally abusive in being manipulative and not giving me what I needed from our relationship. He made me feel inadequate, unattractive and dependent. Prior to our relationship, I was a very independent, confident woman. He took away those things gradually before I knew what was happening. That's how they work.

Kristen: My husband has always been very emotionally abusive and continues to be emotionally abusive. There is never a day that goes by when something is not right. Sadly, at times, I lack the strength to stick up for myself. I hate confrontations and I don't want to make a scene when we're with friends or family. As time goes by, I feel I am getting stronger and am more able to gain more control over these situations and am learning to deal with his negative unacceptable behavior. Through Bonnie's support, I have gained a much better understanding why this type of behavior exists.

Becky: I didn't always see it, but retrospectively, yes he was especially the last 4 years or so.

11. How about the saying, "It's All About Them?" Any comments?

Cheri: This sums up my whole marriage. I did not realize it while living it, but in retrospect, it was always about him. Our whole sex life came down to when he wanted it. His feelings always came first. His opinions were always the right ones. His feelings were the only ones that counted. Although he will never admit to any of this, it all boiled down to keeping things going along peacefully by burying how I felt and giving in to his way of thinking how things should be. Most of our arguments were settled after I gave in, even when I know now that I gave in and compromised my own feelings and emotions to keep him satisfied.

Doomed Grooms

Gretchen: My husband has always been a selfish person; I'm not sure how much the repression of his sexuality has to do with it. It's always been "about him" anyway. Any one who knows him would agree with that.

Carol: Oh my, It Was All About Him from Day ONE. No matter what happened in my life, and still now after two years of divorce, no matter when we speak, then or now, his story is ALL ABOUT HIM. No matter if I got my head cut off, he'd say, "Oh yeah, but, did I tell you this or that?" I could be bleeding to death, his story about himself is much more important (in his mind) than mine and the same is even true with his children!

Michele: It would have to be the truest saying of all. It is all about them, and anything else that happens afterwards that doesn't go right for them is all your fault. They constantly blame others and feel so sorry for themselves. If their love life is good they are happy but if no boyfriend on the scene, well, how can one live life like that with no boyfriend? Very, very selfish.

Syd: Since he's come out, I think this is true. He's had to hide something so deep and for so long; I think that's only normal. They are finding out things about themselves that they never realized before. However, he has been very considerate about my feelings.

Tammy: I could write my own book about this! EVERYTHING has to be about them. In a normal straight relationship, there has to be good, open, honest communication and a lot of give and take. Well, in this gay husband/straight wife relationship, it's NO communication and all TAKE! Gay men are the most selfish people I have ever met. I think that's how they gain so much control of us.

Kristen: To me, this means that when and if your gay spouse if ready to talk or approach the subject of being gay, they will do it when they're ready to do so and it will be on all their own terms and according to their timetable...not yours. Some gay spouses will never ever approach the subject. Gay spouses want to control the whole issue at all times. This is a tough one to cope with. Since finding out my husband is gay, he continues to still outwardly control maintaining the upper hand. Our lives continue in the same way they always have because that's the way my husband wants it to be. He has made a choice not to "come out" in life and therefore, he acts straight to everyone we know, including his work associates, etc. I feel in many ways like he's "buying" my silence by giving me nice gifts, paying household expenses, and taking me on some wonderful vacations. As I stated, he makes a good income and money does indeed talk. I think that it is interesting that at one time, I came home early from work and my husband had obviously been watching one of his gay porn videos. He was terrified that I had caught him and he immediately took the video from the VCR and walked into our bedroom. I walked back to our bedroom and said we needed to talk. He said he was too tired and walked away saying he didn't have time to talk about it. He's never had time to talk about it ever again. I disappoint myself by continuing to tolerate this kind of behavior and never resolve the real issue.

Becky: I didn't always see it, but retrospectively, yes he was especially the last four years or so.

12. What difference has finding and giving support made in your own life?

Cheri: It has made all the difference in the world. Before I found Bonnie, and then the women on the chat, I had no one in my life who I could be totally honest with about all I was feeling and going through in my marriage. Family and friends knew about him being gay, and were there for me in tough times, but could not understand the emotions and different way of life that I lived. My husband and I had a good marriage, we are great friends, but issues came up that I had to deal with on my own. Sometimes I was too embarrassed, or ashamed to share with them. Other times, I felt I had to keep things private to avoid any hard feelings towards my husband in the future when we all got together. Whatever the reasons I felt at the time, I could never be completely open. By sharing with other women who are in various stages of finding out, dealing with a marriage to a gay, or ending the marriage, I find that my self esteem and confidence in myself has grown. I am eternally grateful to each and every one of them, and in the deal, I have made some very good lifelong friends who do not judge me, just stand along side me and accept me for who I am. They have given me the courage to go forward with my life, and see that I am worthy of one day having a relationship with a man who can love me in return the way I have loved my husband. Getting support has given me a purpose in life again. And thanks to having a gay husband, I have found the best friend I ever had in life, Bonnie.

Gretchen: I have found a tremendous amount of comfort in finding many others who share this same journey I do. Everyone's story is a bit different though, so everyone has something different to contribute. When the realization first hit me, I have truly never felt more alone in my life. I now know that I'm not. It also helps me a lot to be able to give advice and perspective to those who are just beginning their journey. Above all, it helps to find some humor in our situation because there are funny things to share and laugh about – no one else is entitled laugh like we can!

Carol: FINDING SUPPORT has, in my opinion, saved my sanity. I live in a very small town in the smallest state where everyone knows everyone, or is related to someone or knows your relatives and I NEVER knew there were so many people going through the same thing. There are probably many people where I live going through the same thing, but, like me, choose not to talk about it. Finding support helped me immensely! I was amazed to find that there were so many people in the same situation.

As for giving support, I was so very fortunate to find support and deemed responsible enough to counsel others. I feel very fortunate to have been so selected. I have tried my VERY best to give the best advice I can give and hope my advice can help others in the same situation. As I tell everyone I speak with, I am certainly not an expert, but I have been down the same road. Maybe I can give them some insight to what is about to come and to know that things will get worse before they get better, not to fool themselves, because they will get worse, but, in the end, things will get better.

If I could have one saying that would fit me, and, from the beginning I have tried to live by, it would be, "Dust yourself off, pick yourself and START ALL OVER AGAIN! So, I guess that's probably my motto!

Michele: It has helped keep me sane. No one really does understand, unless they have been through it. People think they do but they have no idea of the sort of issues that arise. Without it, I don't know where I would have turned for help. Who do you go to and say, "Excuse me, my husband is gay?" So, thank you, Bonnie. You are my light.

Syd: I AM NOT ALONE! It is amazing to me, how many women are going through this. When I know that others are going though this and hurting like I did, I realize, I am not isolated. If there wasn't a Bonnie to help me see that I was OK, I think that would have been much more difficult. Thank you Bonnie ;-)

Tammy: Finding Bonnie and her support group has made all the difference in my life. Through my communication with her and all the women in our support group, I see every week that I am not alone in this situation. All those horrible things I find and face and experience, those things that I thought were so horrible that nobody else could possibly have faced ... THEY HAVE! I think just knowing that someone else has already gone through what you are going through and has come out a better person with a much happier, normal, healthy life gives me the strength, the confidence and the faith in myself to do what I have to do in order to make my life what I want it to be, not what works best for someone else.

Kristen: First of all, I would like to address what difference finding support has made in my life. After discovering my husband was gay, I went to a psychologist that we had both been to several years earlier concerning our marriage. I saw him perhaps six times in one year. It simply came down to: continue to live with the situation or leave your marriage. My psychologist really didn't help me gain a better understanding of the situation, as he himself, was puzzled in knowing what to say. While I had hoped to gain the strength needed to move on in my life, I walked away with more doubts and confusion. I stopped going to therapy after that and continued to "suffer in silence" knowing I was married to a gay spouse. I called our Employee Assistance Program ("EAP") who assists in helping employees deal with situations in life (both work and home related) in hopes of gaining a clearer understanding of what direction to take. They were of no help and couldn't even link me up with a local support group that dealt with gay/straight marriages. I finally found out about a local straight/gay spouse support group after reading a book entitled, "The Other Side of the Closet." After a month, I finally got the nerve to call and check on meeting times, etc. I went to about four meetings. After the second meeting, I knew this group was not for me. The head of the group had and still is married to her gay spouse. She has chosen to stay married to her spouse, but has suffered over the years after watching him nurture his gay relationships and still profess to love her. She had to go to counseling to help resolve some of the many issues she faced on a regular basis and even contemplated suicide at one time due to her spouse being gay and being torn between two lovers—a wife and a gay male lover. The rest of the group participants all had open dialogs with their gay spouses and were in the process of divorces. While I saw myself getting divorced down the road, I had no open dialogs with my husband concerning his gayness nor did I feel I wanted to stay in my marriage forever knowing my husband was and is gay and who also refused to admit being gay then and still does today. So, I felt I was not a good fit for me in continuing to participate in that particular support group. One day, I happened to watch a local TV program and the topic was "Is Your Spouse Gay?" or something like that. Ironically, one of the spouses that were featured happened to be the leader of the support group mentioned above. In addition, people could call in and that's where Bonnie was introduced along with the book she wrote. I felt like the message I was hearing from Bonnie was meant for me. I remember thinking that if Bonnie were a local therapist; I'd surely be knocking on her door. The things that Bonnie said made good sense to me. I immediately went out and bought Bonnie's book. The only obstacle I faced was in not being able to read it in front of my husband. So, I waited until he went to bed and then would pull out the book and read. Once again, things clicked and made perfect sense. Although I was faced with some deep soul searching while reading the book, I felt immediately connected to the things that were being said. I then took advantage of the "one free" counseling session from buying the book and was able to talk personally to Bonnie. She has truly been a saving grace in my life and I have met some wonderful people through her support group. Bonnie has been there for me over the last year and has graciously shared so many valuable insights on no only gay/straight spouse relationships, but so many others lessons in life with me and so many others, too. She is indeed an angel to us all on this earth. I only wished she lived closer; however, I'm confident it's only a matter of time until we get to meet in person.

While I have certainly gotten a lot of support from "our group," I feel that some of my insights and observations have been beneficial to others, as well. Giving support to some of the others makes me feel like I can give back some of what's been given to me. I think we all speak from the heart and at times, our hearts are very heavy. One soon realizes that in giving, we receive a gift ourselves. After knowing Bonnie and being in contact with some of the other group members makes me fully realize that we're not ever alone any longer and we owe it to each other to help support each other though this. When I am among our closest friends and family, I feel like my situation is unique to anything they now face and therefore I do feel very much alone when I'm among them. By choice, I have not let our closest friends know my situation. Whenever I have a chance to reach out to others in our group, it also helps me. Helping support others helps make me stronger. I believe in searching for answers to other questions, we gain new knowledge and insight with each new day and we hopefully continue to grow stronger in finding out the right path to our own inner peace and happiness along the way. I dearly love being a part of this group and feel privileged to know Bonnie in my life. I am humbly grateful for all she's done to help me in gaining a much greater understanding of a gay/straight marriage and she has helped make me a better and stronger person as I face the challenges ahead. She has also helped remind me not to forget about taking care of me along the way. Sadly, somewhere in my life, I've forgotten to do this.

Becky: I have only just found support specifically for this situation in the last 10 months. Wow, has it felt good and helped me to understand some of the reasons for my ex's actions and comments. When I first discovered others who had been in the same situation, I couldn't get enough. The common descriptions of things I had been told and things I had felt was amazing. I wonder if it has made it easier to let go of some of the feelings and mystery. To be able to tell someone "I understand" or "don't be surprised if......" does have some way of improving your feeling of isolation. I think the isolation is the **worst** side effect of this whole situation.

The Men Who Help Me
Make A Difference

I have been very blessed to meet two wonderful men who have made a significant difference in my life and thinking. These men, Jay and Chuck, found me through my website and wrote to me in support of my work. These are two men who have as opposite of an upbringing as two people can have. Jay was raised in a Jewish family in Philadelphia; Pennsylvania, and Chuck was raised as a Christian fundamentalist in Mississippi. Even though their lives were so different geographically, religiously, and culturally, their experiences and thoughts parallel each other in so many ways.

These are gay men who grew up in an environment of little tolerance for homosexuality. Both of them went through the expected life events of getting married and having families. Both of them realized at some point during their marriage that no matter how hard they tried to be straight, they were gay. Neither one of them wanted to hurt his wife. They loved their wives when they decided to marry and had the same dreams that straight men have. As the years went on and the attraction to men increased, not decreased, they knew they had to deal with the fact that they are homosexual.

We have all learned from each other since our friendships began. Jay and Chuck have been sensitized to the pain that women go through when they learn about homosexuality in the marriage. I have been made much more aware of the personal struggle and pain that gay men go through while coming to terms with their homosexuality.

Both Jay and Chuck have helped me clarify a lot of my thinking. They have inspired me to find new words and thoughts that I have written about in my newsletters and in this book. They keep me focused when I become jaded from too many letters of sadness from women who are suffering. They have offered their time and support to many men who have written to me in their struggle to come to terms with their homosexuality, as well as confused women who need help in understanding their husbands. They share their own personal stories with others to give them understanding, hope and inspiration.

What I like best about both of these men is that they don't feel the need to change their thoughts in order to find acceptance within the gay community. They feel secure enough within themselves to offer a point of view that makes sense based on fairness. They know these are imperfect circumstances and there's no way to perfect them and make them into something they can't be.

I asked these two friends if they would answer questions that would give better insight to straight wives and gay husbands who are desperately searching for answers. They were gracious enough to say "yes." Here is some background information about them and their answers.

JAY

JAY'S PERSONAL INFORMATION:

I am a forty-nine-year-old father of two children. I am Jewish. I live in a small city in Pennsylvania where I practice law. I was married to the mother of my children for 22 years. My daughter is a college student who is twenty, and my son is seventeen. I ended my marriage to their mother in September of 1996 depressed, distraught and believing that I might well spend the remainder of my life alone and closeted.

I had struggled with my sexual orientation for much of the preceding decade. Even though I was not dating and had few gay friends, rumors within our community began that I had left my wife for another man. I was shocked and angry....perhaps

153

more so because it could have happened that way. In any event, at the urging of my best friend I went on a date, awoke the next morning, racked with guilt and asking myself what I was doing going out on a date with a woman.

Not long thereafter in the spring of 1997 I was introduced to a man who would become my spouse. He shared my path in that he was a divorced father with two sons only slightly older than my children. I was lucky. I found my soulmate. He saw me through my coming out to my children, extended family and friends. He was there to challenge me to resolve my differences with my ex-wife, so that she, the children and we could move on. We were married in the first same-sex ceremony to be conducted in the oldest synagogue in our city. It is my hope that in living my life openly and publicly making clear our relationship I can set an example for the next generation of young gay men and women. I also believe that the public visibility of my journey is bound to have opened the eyes of some straight young adults to question the orientation of their partners prior to marriage.

JAY'S ANSWERS TO MY QUESTIONS:

1. At what age did you start to think about same-sex attractions?

A. I am not certain when I first became aware of same-sex attractions per se. However, I recall thinking that I was "different" from other boys as early as the age of five. I was interested in activities that did not fit the gender stereotypes of the fifties. I was born in 1952. I was interested in art and recall drawing in the sand in my backyard long before I could write. My mother tells me that I loved listening to classical music and would ask for it as a preschooler. I played with my sister's dolls and chose to sleep in the extra bed in her bedroom rather than the room I shared with my younger brother. I must have been somewhat effeminate in my demeanor, since I have vivid memories of being scolded by my mother for "yelling like a girl" when I was seven.

154

When I was about ten or eleven, I remember a boy in my class whom I admired and sought out opportunities to be in his company. At the time, I did not identify this attraction as sexual. I thought I wanted to be like him and felt good when he paid attention to me. I even signed up for little league because he did, although I had neither an interest nor any ability in athletics.

2. Prior to the time of marriage, did you consider yourself gay?

A. I did not consider myself gay at the time. I had only ever dated women and had never had a sexual relationship with another male.

3. Had you acted on your homosexuality prior to marriage?

A. No.

4. Did you think that getting married would "eliminate" those feelings for men?

A. I was not able to even articulate to myself that my interest in other males was sexual at the time. I knew I "admired" other men, but rationalized it much as I had as a child....that these were men I would like to be or look like. In retrospect, by armor of denial was indeed very strong. For me, getting married was what I always thought and hoped for. I wanted a family, loved children and loved my wife.

She had been my very best friend in college. Indeed, we built the very life I thought we would. She helped me through law school and I supported her getting a Masters Degree in Social Work. We overcame infertility problems to have two children, a girl and a boy. We were active in our community and involved in our synagogue.

I am sure it looked to all as though we were the All American family. However, over time I came to focus on all that was wrong with our relationship and awakened and became more open to confronting my same-sex attractions.

5. When you were getting married, did you think that sexual activity would be a problem between you and your wife?
A. I was barely twenty-one when I married. At that time, even a swift breeze would arouse me. Moreover, my wife was inexperienced sexually and initially praised me a lot with respect to our lovemaking. It was not until a couple years after our marriage that sexual dreams and fantasies of men began for me. I think that the freer I became sexually with my wife, the freer I was to begin breaking free of my own armor and allow myself to picture what I needed and wanted. However, none of this happened swiftly for me or without tremendous guilt and self-admonition.

6. Did you feel that if you discussed some of your doubts or previous experiences with your future wife she would understand?
A. I once raised my fears in response to teasing from my wife about my lack of interest in sports and the like. It was never openly discussed again until after we separated. I did not feel she would understand or want to know.

7. Did you think that you could be monogamous within the marriage at the time that you married?
A. I married thinking that we would raise a family and grow old together. I was not interested in or particularly attracted to other women, so I thought monogamy would be easy.

8. Did you ever "enjoy" sexual relations with your wife?
A. As I said before, our sexual relationship was a good one which I enjoyed. It became more difficult as I had more to hide and the relationship deteriorated.

9. Did you find it natural or unnatural to be making love to a woman? Were there aspects of the sexuality that you weren't comfortable with?

A. Sex with my wife felt natural because it was what I knew. Having married quite young and having begun to have sex with a woman in response to my own arousal, perhaps I did not realize that the arousal was not triggered by her physically. Surely love had a lot to do with my sexual performance with her. It was not until I had sex with a man that I realized how "natural" sex could feel.

10. How what point in your marriage did you have sexual relations with a man?
A. I was marred for ten years before I had my first sexual experience with a man.

11. Did you consider it "cheating" when you did, or did you "justify" it at the time as not cheating?
A. I rationalized that it was not cheating because it was not with another woman, but I did feel it was dishonest, felt guilty, remorseful and vowed not to do it again. When I did do it again, I secretly went to a 'therapist'. The therapist was not very skillful and probably was not credentialed. She suggested that I was not gay as I feared, but rather acting out because of the tension and distress in my marriage. I knew in my heart she was wrong and ceased therapy. I should have sought a better therapist. Years later, I did.

12. Did you feel a sense of frustration by being in a marriage with a woman?
A. I was frustrated with my wife in particular and focused on the many ways in which we were in conflict and all of her shortcomings as a wife, mother and homemaker. Since I did not come out until after we separated, I was incapable of identifying my unhappiness as a function of being gay. After the divorce, I married another man. What is remarkable is how many of the things that drove me crazy with my ex-wife do not seem so important in the context of my same-sex marriage. The point is that I was not capable of identifying my frustration

at being in a marriage to a woman while I was in it, but obviously I was.

13. Did your wife "sense" your frustration?

A. I have no doubt that my wife knew I was frustrated, but I doubt that she knew what was at the root of much of it.

14. How did you eventually come out to your wife? Did she suspect anything prior to the time you told her?

A. I came out to my wife when she confronted me with questions my children had begun asking about me. She had figured it out by then.

15. How did your wife react when the truth was learned?

A. My wife was angry but controlled. She felt I had deceived her. One of her first questions was whether she needed to be tested for AIDS. Notwithstanding her anger and feelings of deception and abandonment, she agreed to be present when I came out to our children who were 12 and 15 at the time.

16. Do your children know about your being gay? How are they handing it?

A. Like many men who finally decide to come out, I was driven by a quest for honesty in my life and a desire to rebuild what I lost. My children never stopped loving me, did not reject me as I had feared prior to coming out to them, but they were fairly angry about how it changed their lives for the first few years. As a consequence, I had to be persistent in staying in their lives and reminding them that I would always be their dad and love them no matter how angry they may be or unresponsive.

They needed time and I needed to recognize that they needed to deal with their own 'coming out' as the child of a gay parent. Six years later, our relationships are strong. They have even accepted my partner as step-parent and seem to think of his children as extended family. We are not the gay Brady

Bunch I once imagined we could be, but we now share mutual respect, love and support. What more can one ask?

17. In retrospect, if you could turn back the hands of time, is there anything you would have done differently?
A. If I could do things differently, I would have come out to my ex-wife sooner and trusted her to work through the journey with me. I know that we would still have divorced but we might have salvaged the beautiful friendship which first brought us together. As for my children, I would take things slower, push less and be quicker to recognize their need for time and experience with other gay people to grow in comfort. For my new spouse, I would insist that we take things slower not only so that he would have been less the focus of the children's anger, but so that I would have been further out...as a gay man and... out of a protracted angry divorce.

18. Have you found the fulfillment your were seeking in life with another man?
A. Yes.

19. Is it much different than your relationship with your wife?
A. I am different than I was when I was married to a woman. I am not secretive, so I do not feel under scrutiny. My feelings are not chaotic, so I do not demand order in my environment to help me feel in control. I do not live in fear of discovery, so I am able to express anger without fear of losing control. I have experienced the intolerance of others directed at me, so I am more tolerant of others, including my same-sex spouse. I am less rigid, so I am more flexible with my same-sex spouse.

20. If you could give some advice to men who are "stuck" in this situation and don't know which way to turn, what would you tell them?

A. I would challenge them to face what they do know. I do not think that men who are stuck do not know which way to turn. Rather, they are stuck because of the fear of the unknown and fear of losing what they think they have. There are indeed losses, many of which are wrenching and sad. There is the loss of the dreams one shared with your spouse. There is the loss of daily contact with children. There is the loss of acquaintances or so-called friends and the loss of respect in some quarters of the community. But there is the opportunity to grow and live and love with integrity and the opportunity to experience the love of family and friends who want to understand. There is the opportunity to become more trusting. These opportunities are priceless.

21. What would you tell the wives of gay husbands who are struggling to make sense of this situation?
A. Your life will forever be different than you imagined, but it need not be bad. Your husband is taking care of himself. You need to take care of yourself. You did not make him gay. He may not have wanted to deceive you. He loved you and entered the marriage full of the love, hope and plans for the future you shared. What was good in your relationship really happened. Your husband cannot change his orientation. His secret undermined the trust in your relationship. There can be no relationship in the absence of trust. You deserve better. Grieve for the loss of what you expected. Strive to recognize what you really had and what you did not. Work to move on. There are straight men out there whom you can trust and provide you with the love and passion to which you are entitled.

CHUCK

CHUCK'S PERSONAL INFORMATION:

I am 59 years old, married now for 30 years with three wonderful children, a daughter now 30, a son who is 18 and a daughter who died at age 2 in 1976.

My wife is a long-term elementary school teacher and I am an Administrator of a mental retardation facility in the Deep South. My wife and my surviving children know of my sexual orientation. They are accepting and as understanding as anyone could be with so many diverse opinions about sexual orientation. Out of respect for my children and because my sexual orientation does not define who I am, I am discreet [closeted] in my profession and my community life. I think it's unfair to expect my children to try to "explain away" their gay dad when I don't have all the answers to "why and how" myself.

1. At what age did you start to think about same-sex attractions?
A. I can't remember when I wasn't attracted to men. Even before puberty, there were older men who were attractive to me and I can remember wishing they would hold me, snuggle with me. I can't remember ever being sexually or physically attracted to a female.... well, maybe Marilyn Monroe one time. <smile>

2. Prior to the time of marriage, did you consider yourself gay?
A. Yes, but because of my spiritual upbringing, I thought it was something that could be changed if I were just "spiritual" enough.

3. Had you acted on your homosexuality prior to marriage?
A. Yes! Didn't marry until I was 27.

4. Did you think that getting married would "eliminate" those feelings for men?
A. I had never had sex with a female when I married so I thought that perhaps, just perhaps, once I did, the sex and God would take the sinful lustful desires for men away from me. (I was ignorant and deceived at the time.)

5. When you were getting married, did you think that sexual activity would be a problem between you and your wife?
A. I counseled with a married bisexual friend before marriage because I feared that I would not be able to have sex with my bride. He assured me that sex with his wife was fulfilling and that I would enjoy it and it would be no problem. Again, I was ignorant about gays, bisexuality, etc., and accepted his counsel.

Also, I mistakenly thought that women didn't like sex and that my wife wouldn't expect it so I would be "safe".

6. Did you feel that if you discussed some of your doubts or previous experiences with your future wife she would understand?
A. NO way! How could SHE understand when I didn't understand it myself? And remember, I thought it was just a "sinful behavior" because I wasn't spiritual enough and therefore, felt that I would eventually overcome it by "drawing night to God". Also, at that time, [the 50s and 60s], I thought I was perhaps the only fundamentalist Christian in the world having this conflict and no one would be able to understand. Since my faith considered same sex activity "the worst of sins", I could never confide my "secret" to anyone other than gay men I met, and even those, spiritual issues related to our sexuality, was rarely discussed.

7. Did you think that you could be monogamous within the marriage at the time that you married?
A. Yes, I thought that God would change me for "doing right by getting married to a wonderful, Christian woman" and that my

desires for men would leave me as I grew in my love for her and God.

8. Did you ever "enjoy" sexual relations with your wife?
A. Sadly, for her, NO. It was an act of endurance each time and I truly hated that it was because my wife enjoyed it, deserved it and wanted it. After my honeymoon (where I thought I should be the aggressor--it was the expected thing to do) all sexual activity between us was initiated by her.

9. Did you find it natural or unnatural to be making love to a woman? Were there aspects of the sexuality that you weren't comfortable with?
A. Very unnatural. Even the intimacy was uncomfortable. It felt strange to me to even hold hands.

10. How what point in your marriage did you have sexual relations with a man?
A. The desire was strong and I couldn't get away from it, regardless of praying and begging God to take it away. I would go to "pick up" places for anonymous sex with no intimacy.

11. Did you consider it "cheating" when you did, or did you "justify" it at the time as not cheating?
A. I justified it. Since I was not seeing other women, I considered myself faithful to my wife. To me, it was in the same category as masturbating-a private sexual relief, except it was more enjoyable. Of course, even masturbating was considered wrong and sinful in my faith at that time so this drove me to remain closeted.

12. Did you feel a sense of frustration by being in a marriage with a woman?
A. Absolutely. It wasn't until many years into my marriage that I was able to understand that I took out my frustrations on my wife. I belittled her, tried to make her dislike me so she wouldn't

163

want sex   and intimacy. Because I   disliked   myself   and what I was doing, I passed that frustration on to her and made her life miserable.

13. Did your wife "sense" your frustration?
A. Yes, she was the object of my frustrations most time.

14. How did you eventually come out to your wife? Did she suspect anything prior to the time you told her?
A. My wife learned that I had sexual attractions to men a few months before we married. We were both naive, ignorant about sexuality, and sincerely dedicated to our faith. We both thought that being obedient to God by getting married [because that was God's will for men and women] would end my attraction to men. I was also getting counseling for a Christian Psychiatrist at the time who believed that sex with her was what I needed.

15. How did your wife react when the truth was learned?
A. She was hurt! Felt I had deceived her. Disappointed in my "lack of spirituality", my lack of "being the spiritual head of the household", my manly responsibility. We were both still ignorant about sexual orientation so she took my actions very personally as an affront to her.

16. Do your children know about your being gay? How are they handing it?
A. I have two surviving children. One is 30 and one is 18. Both know in the past two years that I am gay. My daughter and I openly discuss it. My son "could care less" as he's so involved with his girlfriends, peers, etc. We even joke about it sometimes together. We are comfortable with it. My wife isn't.

My greatest fear in life was that I would loose them over my sexual orientation. One of my daughters had died and the grief from her death almost destroyed me. I didn't think I could survive losing another child - even via estrangement - so the coming out process was totally in consideration for them, not myself.

I didn't want my teenage son to have to explain to his friends that he had a "queer dad". My remaining in the closet was to protect them. I have never "flaunted" my sexual orientation and never will. Other than being attracted to men, I am just like any other man. I attend and have been very active in church, organizations, do volunteer work, take care of my family financially, and enjoy them.

17. In retrospect, if you could turn back the hands of time, is there anything you would have done differently?
A. My children are my gifts in life. When I think about what my life would have been without them had I lived an openly gay lifestyle and not married, it wouldn't have been worth it. I continually thank my wife for giving this "gift" to me even through all the pain that we have caused each other.

Would I do anything differently? I regret that I didn't become educated about sexual orientation at a younger age. I lived many years of frustration tying to make my "desires fit into my spiritual teachings" before I realized that my spiritual teachings were wrong all these years. I came to accept myself and find my peace with God about my sexuality late in life, after many people were hurt. Perhaps I could have saved some of the hurt. But would I have preferred to life a single life within the gay community? Absolutely NOT! Having a family, especially children, has been so fulfilling for me. My heart goes out to gays, etc., who miss the experience of unconditional love that comes from your children. Without it, it's difficult to understand how God our Father/Mother could love us, His/Her children, so unconditionally. I am blessed! I am grateful! I am thankful!

Do I wish that gays could live openly? ABSOLUTELY! Everyone should be able to love and be loved without fear of condemnation. Until that day comes however, I feel I have an obligation to consider those that love me and those that I love in my actions and lifestyle. Doing so is not being a traitor to the gay rights agenda. When it comes to agenda vs. the ones I love, the ones I love win every time.

18. Have you found the fulfillment your were seeking in life with another man? Is it much different than your relationship with your wife?
A. I accepted my sexuality and found my peace with God about 8 years ago, in my early 50s. Once I did this, I was free to experience intimacy with another man rather than just have sexual encounters. But, I learned that I was immature and inexperienced in managing relationships. I fell in love with every guy who was nice to me <smile>. I was just now learning things about relationships that most people learn as teenagers. I also learned that there ere gay men who were deeply spiritual and this thrilled me since I had been taught all my life that the two couldn't possibly exist. My relationships moved from "pick ups" for sexual gratification to loyalty to one man with whom I could enjoy things other than sex. I have found fulfillment that I never dreamed possible with the man that I've been seeing for almost two years now. We do not live together [yet] and both have families and similar experiences with acceptance and struggling to find meaning and purpose in our lives. It's a daily learning experience for us to "try to do the right things" for our wives and children now and lessen the hurt that we've caused and received. The connection of the souls is more than I deserve and I am thankful. However, to know that I have caused my wife to miss out on this all these years is an ongoing act of repentance for me.

19. If you could give some advice to men who are "stuck" in this situation and don't know which way to turn, what would you tell them?
A. They must accept themselves and become at peace with who they are so they can make sense of their journeys. Then, and only then, can they make decisions that affect them and their families in a compassionate, logical, caring manner.

20. What would you tell the wives of gay husbands who are struggling to make sense of this situation?

A. "Don't take it personally." This is not a rejection of you as a wife, a woman, a person. And, you will not be able to change a gay husband into a straight one. Educate yourself on the issues and be as objective as you can so you can find your peace and move on with your life. Try to avoid hate between the two of you. It's not anyone's fault. Don't take and don't place blame.

A Final Note
to the Gay Husband

I believe that the most difficult deed a gay married man must do in his life is to come out to his wife. I am not paying lip service to this monumental life changing decision. I know it has to be frightening for any man who loves his wife and family. Perhaps this is why so many men don't do it. It's fear—fear of losing everything that is important and secure in life. Lots of people live without being happy, but they trade it off for a sense of security and stability. Stability in this case means knowing what to expect every day of your life from the family you live with even if it isn't fulfilling.

Through the years, I have watched thousands of gay men struggle with this decision, and I have guided them into making the only conscionable decision that can be made—namely, coming out.

It has been so interesting working with men who refuse to tell their wives, claiming that this kind of catastrophic news will only destroy the lives of their wives. Their wives are happy— why upset the applecart? Those are the men who are too afraid of the consequences for themselves, not their wives. Those are the men who will keep blaming their wives for their unhappiness throughout the marriage, looking to find fault with them and pick, pick, pick, until there's a great big sore growing that will at best form a scab but never heal.

I have advocated from my earliest writings nearly 30 years ago that a man has an obligation to tell this information to his wife. In my nationally syndicated column "Straight Talk" in the mid 1980's, I wrote these words in my column titled "Come Out To Your Wife" which still ring true today:

168

Marriage is the highest form of commitment a man can make with a woman. It supersedes all prior relationships and goes beyond friendship. The person you marry lives with you on a day-to-day basis and shares your life—the good times and bad, during sickness and health, through your moments of glory and depths of despair. It is a relationship built on trust and honesty towards each other. That is not to say that every move in a marriage must be explained. Sooner or later we all fall into the trap of making up "little white lies;" however, hiding your homosexuality is not exactly keeping a little secret when it plays such a big role in your life. It is living a lie. You are living a double life in two separate worlds, and the twain will never meet. There is another side of you that is totally hidden from the person who has so much trust in you and relies on you for basic honesty.

As I have come to learn in the years since I have written this, there's a lot more to it than just the issue of honesty. There is also the bigger picture of the mental atrophy women go through when they are unknowingly married to a gay man.

Now, I am NOT saying that most gay husbands are intentionally cruel to their wives. But when you're somewhere you don't want to really be or don't really belong, those little winces that show on your face become a message over time— your wife is doing something wrong to make you unhappy. Yep, that's what we think. And then it moves to the next stage of constant self-questioning of "Why am I failing at being a good wife? No matter what I do, I can't make him happy." And then it moves across the house to the bedroom where we start wondering, "Why aren't I enough of a woman to please him? How come he doesn't want to make love to me, or when he does, it feels as if he's doing me a favor?" And so on, and so on.

You see, it's not just the basic lie any more or the fact of keeping an important truth from your life mate. It's the stripping down of her self-esteem, her sexual esteem, and her very sense of self-worth by hiding this information. It's definitely not good. This is why the truth has to be told. It will never be easy, palatable, or acceptable, but it has to be done anyway.

Some of the men I have worked with felt the pain of their wives. I would like to share some of their thoughts with you to give you insight into their thinking. Perhaps if you are a gay man, you can understand this pain. If you are a straight wife, hopefully you can see the struggle that some of the husbands go through. I have anonymously reprinted the words of five men who shared their struggle with me.

I am married to a wonderful woman and don't know if I am truly bisexual or even gay. You make it sound so easy in your website to tell your wife, but really it's just tearing me apart. She knows that I'm not happy but doesn't know why. Hoping that your chapter on bisexuality will maybe help me to understand how to move on in my life.

I have recently told my wife that I am bisexual. We are wondering how we can carry on in our lives and move forward, if at all? We have three young children. My wife feels she has lost her self-respect now for not realizing that I was Bisexual. I, too, am feeling unworthy and uncomfortable that my wife knows and now has to put up with knowing. I don't want to hurt her anymore than she is already. Do you have any advice on how my wife can get her self-respect back and anything else that we may find useful? Thanks for what you are doing....

You asked, "Why now at this particular time?" Actually the answer is pretty much in your next paragraph, "The husband is frustrated after a period of time because the relationship can never fulfill the needs that the man has." That applies to sex but more than that the emotional bond that hopefully exists between 2 people who are partners. You made a reference to what I mean in one of your newsletters. You were talking about your own experience in your new relationship. It's the difference between having sex and making love. My wife and I have a strong emotional bond and we have sex but I know the emotional bond we enjoy with each other is on a lower level than what can exist if there was a true sexual attraction. That's what I know I need to be "fulfilled".

Of course I know that's a two way street. Although she may not realize it, that kind of fulfillment is missing from her life as well. We can be each other's best friend, have a decent sex life, but I can't fake the real emotional giving to that level in a straight relationship. And I know she deserves better.

I guess the reason it's finally happening now is really just a matter of being able to finally acknowledge my own sexuality combined with where I'm at in life age-wise. I'm 44 (she's 38).I feel like I've just wasted the first half of my life (I realize that's thinking in purely selfish terms),and if I go on this way I'll either go insane, commit suicide or reach the end of my life and realize that I've wasted the whole thing. Yes, I know she may want to stay married and try to work things out. I won't lie to you, I look forward to living on the other side.

But I'm committed to working through this first, whatever it takes. If we can somehow get through this and remain best or at least good friends, I will consider myself the luckiest person in the world.

Bonnie, thank you so much for what you do. I hope you can believe me when I say my #1 concern is to cause the least amount of pain to my best friend, my wife. I want to do the right thing. Please, if you have any other advice.

I realize that it is critical for me to be completely honest and open with her, and I am trying to be, but every time I approach the subject from a standpoint of "I cannot go on ignoring this,

this is who I am becoming," she retorts with her profound love and need for me and me alone, and compounds it all with thinly veiled treats of suicide. I know her to be a strong woman, whom I admire greatly, but I cannot continue addressing my sexuality and its impact on our relationship if she makes these kinds of statements. I still care deeply about her and her well-being - how can I be who I am if it threatens her health, or even life?

I am a gay man who was married for 18 years. I was actually one of the ones who didn't "experiment" with other men while I was married. However, lack of activity didn't reduce my desire to fulfill a part of my life that was lacking. I felt a keen sense of agreement with you on most of your points in the book, particularly your view that bisexuality is basically an illusion.

I am sorry that you were hurt by your gay husband. I am sure that he loved you in his own way, and I know I loved my wife. It is unfortunate that we live in a society that intelligent caring people will make decisions that deep inside our hearts we must know seems wrong, but we feel we have no other acceptable choice. I am glad you have found happiness with someone with whom you can enjoy the sexual pleasure as well as that missing intimacy that you must have missed in your second marriage. I always wanted it, and never seemed that I could attain it until I met my current partner a few months after I separated from my wife.

We have been together a little over 3 years, and have yet to have a serious disagreement. I had been convinced after an 18 year turbulent marriage that happiness would always be beyond my grasp, but not I know that was only true because I was trying to find it with a person who would not be able to meet all of my needs through no fault of her own.

We are now cooperating on the raising of our two teenage sons, and while we do not agree on the acceptance of my homosexuality due to deep-seated religious prejudice on her part, we have put that to the side to be positive with our children.

I appreciate you for writing your book because I believe it is truth that needs to be revealed to both gay men, and women who might be attracted to them. Hopefully, your book will keep a gay man from going down the misguided path of marriage in hopes that his homosexual desires will fade -- they don't as you and I painfully know.

I wish you well in your life and counseling practice.

As you can see from the letters, these gay husbands do care about the mental well being of their wives because they love them. These are honest men who realize that they can never love a woman they way she needs and deserves to be loved. And because they love them, they believe that coming out is the only right thing to do. Of course, these are men who are honest with themselves. They are not the "Limbo Men" or "Straight Gay Men" who are dishonest or unable to accept their homosexuality. But for many of us who are/were married to gay men who do come to terms with themselves, these men give us some comfort because they express feelings of husbands who have these genuine concerns about the well-being of their wives.

Gay husbands must come to realize that their journey has taken a lifetime to reach the point of where they are ready to accept themselves. They **cannot** and **should not** expect that their wives will be able to adjust to this information overnight, in a week, or in a month. They need to give their wives adequate time to make the necessary adjustments to this life changing news.

Remember men—while your life as you know it is about to end and your are filled with excitement and anticipation, your wife's life as she knew it is also about to end—but with sadness and a great sense of loss. While you will spend the upcoming months and years exploring your new lifestyle, she will spend the same time finding herself again and building up the confidence that has been knocked down. Your inward struggle is now over while your wife's is just beginning. She may finally understand what the real problem was in the marriage, but she will still question herself in many ways.

Men have asked me what they can do to make this easier on their wives. I give them ALL the same answer—**DO THE RIGHT THING.** Be responsible to your family. Give them the emotional and financial support that they need. Put the needs of your children above your own personal needs and ego. Give your wife the proper time to make adjustments and mourn the marriage. And many wives mourn their marriage because they love their husbands so much. Give her time to adjust and don't make her feel uncomfortable. There is nothing more hurtful to a straight wife than seeing her husband with another man. This takes time. Don't throw your new happiness or your new lover in her face.

You can't be her lover—but you can be her friend. If you have children together, you can be her co-parent. Put yourself in her shoes and see how you would feel. If it doesn't feel comfortable, don't do it.

Most of all—learn to say that you're sorry. You're not sorry for being gay. That is something that you had no choice in. And you're not sorry for marrying her because you loved her enough to believe it could work. But at least be sorry now that it's over that the dreams you had together will never come true. And make sure you let her know that she is not to blame for your homosexuality or the failure of your marriage. That's the first step to a viable friendship for the future.

Where I Stand
and What I've Learned

I've been immersed in the field of straight/gay relationships for nearly thirty years. I have spoken to and worked over 75,000 women who find themselves in this situation. I have also worked with over two thousand gay men who need guidance on how to reveal this information to their wives and how to proceed afterwards.

In almost all of the stories that I have witnessed, couples find themselves wasting valuable years of their lives trying to make something work that was a mistake. I've coined the phrase **"mismarriages"** to describe these marriages. It simply means—a marriage that was a mistake. It happens all of the time in situations that don't have the complication of homosexuality. And people cut their losses all of the time and move on to a better place and space in life. It's easy to make a mistake when you are younger. But it just seems so difficult for people to "fix" the problem when they are older.

Some people look at their failed marriages as their personal failures. I see this happen often when there have been previous marriages. Women feel they failed the first time and think that giving up on a second or third marriage is their failure. They look for reasons to justify keeping this mistake together just so they don't have to admit defeat again. Ugh. It's like moving from the fire pan into the fire and deciding that living life fried like a burnt egg is their destiny. Double ugh. Where is the pot of gold over the rainbow here? All you can see in front of you is a pot of dirty ashes. Is there any point to this? No, none at all. Prolonging a disastrous relationship makes absolutely no sense to me at all.

I have learned that some women will look for any excuse not to accept their husbands' homosexuality. They believe that their marriage will be the miracle marriage that will revert back to where it once was before the thoughts of gay entered their psyche. These women write to me with condemning words, telling me that I don't know what I'm talking about. Ummm....I think I do. Sometimes, they are kind enough to write me a letter of apology weeks, months, and even years later for thinking I was the voice of doom. I know that being the voice of reason and sanity is a tough job, but someone has to do it, and I'm willing to take on the job.

I believe that women who marry gay men for the most part are the kindest, most giving, caring women in the world. I don't think that it is an accident that this happens. Gay men gravitate toward women who have these qualities because they know in their hearts that someday, even if they haven't come to understand their homosexuality at the time of their marriage, something may happen that will create a need to be with a woman whose empathy will overshadow her own needs of happiness and well being.

I have seen women sacrifice their own happiness and give up years of valuable time because their love for their husbands supersede their love for themselves. They live with their hurt wrapped up tightly in their chest often causing a sense of suffocation because they want their husbands to love them as much as they love men. Even when their husbands tell them the truth, they won't let go. They can't let go. They just keep trying harder and harder to make something happen that will never happen.

I have learned that trust is slow in returning after you have been married to a gay man. The kinds of trust that are lacking are both trust of self and trust of men. We have had our sense of trust stripped and peeled layer by layer and it takes a lot of time to rebuild this. We wonder how we could have been "duped" for so long, not understanding how we married gay men. What did we miss? How couldn't we tell? Why didn't we see the signs—if not first, then through the years? We question ourselves for hours during the days and years ahead. We are very hard on ourselves and don't easily trust our sense of judgment for a long time.

We have trust issues in our future relationships. We made a major mistake once; will we make that same mistake again? Sometimes this lack of trusts stops us from having fulfilling relationships with our new partners. They become easy targets of suspicion because we can't help to suspect. I know that it took me years to trust my soulmate because I lacked trust in myself. I needed constant reassurance, and sometimes, no matter how hard he tried, I still had the seeds of doubt growing. This means that if you are going to have a successful relationship in the future, you will need to find a man who is as exceptionally understanding towards you as you were with your gay husband. He needs to understand your issues so you need to communicate.

I have learned that communication is the key factor in a relationship. We have to be able to communicate our feelings and desires even if we were conditioned not to ask for anything while we were married. So many of us were tired of being rebuffed by our gay husbands and made to feel that the problems in our marriages were OUR fault. When our husbands made us feel that we could never be good wives, we started not to ask for anything in the marriage for fear of being "bad wives." Truth be told, the majority if us were the best wives. We kept trying to please our husbands and even though they seemed to have no interest in us, we kept trying harder hoping they could love us better. Nothing worked. It couldn't. Our husbands were gay.

Now that we have relationships with straight men, we still fear that feeling of rejection so we just don't bother to express what we want. We want our new men to be mind readers and just know what we are thinking, but then feel rejection when they have no clue what we are upset about. Ouch. That hurts when they just don't know. You have to learn to express your feelings without fear of criticism. This is what makes a relationship successful. Trust has to be earned, but you have to give it a chance without always showing doubt.

On the other hand, I have seen women jump into new relationships with straight men that are mistakes and even abusive for fear of being alone. They are repeating their same pattern of mistakes just with a different man who also will never be able to treat them with respect and love. I believe that after a marriage is over, it takes time to rebuild yourself. You must do an honest self-evaluation of how your marriage affected you and your sense of self-worth while working on building your self-esteem. These are not easy tasks and take lots of time to conquer.

I used to think that self-esteem was based on looks. Having been an overweight person all of my life, my sense of self-esteem was never as high as it needed to be or deserved to be. One great lesson I have learned is that size, color, and shape have no bearing on self-esteem. I have seen the most beautiful women of model quality end up in the same situation as I am in. And their sense of self-esteem is often lower than mine. I have worked with incredible women who are doctors, attorneys, stockbrokers, models, actresses, psychologists, professors, and even elected politicians who have met with the same fate as the rest of us. Their sense of self-esteem was no higher than mine either. It shows me that even women who started out with a strong sense of self-worth can be ripped down and shredded like the rest of us. Destruction of the inner soul has no boundaries.

I have heard the saddest stories from women who truly are trapped by cultural walls. These are women from other countries where the blame is immediately placed on them if their husbands are gay. These women are truly doomed. Their lives are being sacrificed because they have no chance of happiness or escape. There is nowhere for them to run or hide.

On the other hand, I have seen women who have all the resources and the luxury of freedom who don't have the physical walls of entrapment, but they are just as trapped by the psychological walls. The mental chains keep them immobilized and unable to move in any direction. Guess what? I make no judgment on women who are paralyzed into inaction. Every woman has to move at her own pace and in her own comfort zone. Some women, unfortunately, will never make it to the finish line. Their golden years will be wasted and turned into mudslide years, drowning in the muck. And the golden years aren't the older years—they are the prime time years when women had the opportunity to find the love of a straight man—or even just the love of themselves. When you stay in a marriage with a gay man, you lose the ability to love yourself because you are too busy trying to make him love you.

I believe in my heart that gay men in almost all cases love the women they marry. It is not their intention to "fool" us or "trick" us when they marry us. However, as the years pass, many of them forget that love as the need to be who they are surfaces and starts to bloom. I have seen the most loving of husbands and fathers become creatures of the unknown. For some, it is a phase—for others it is a permanent lifestyle. The women who were there to share their pain and hurt now are their enemies. Their sense of responsibility to the family goes down the drain. They not only chose a new lifestyle with their sexuality, but also with their irresponsibility when it came to the wife and family.

I also know that this is not a trait that's exclusive to gay men. I have seen many straight men take the same road. They remarry, have new families, and forget their old ones. They become exemplary fathers to their new children and forget about the ones they left behind. I don't get it—I'll never get it.

On the other hand, I know there are wonderful gay fathers who are responsible to their children and their ex-wives. I've met them and I admire them. Their families always come first before their own needs, or at least most of the time. I can't say that I have seen them as the majority, but I have seen them. I greatly admire these men for having their priorities "straight."

I have seen women whose lives have been destroyed by the lies of their gay husbands. But I have also come to learn—and believe—that gay men themselves often don't even understand that they are lying. They are keeping one step ahead of themselves with their lies. They keep spinning the webs thinking that they are covering themselves, when, in fact, they are just strangling their wives with these traps. They justify it by saying that they are living their own hells, but for some reason, they think their wives are shatter proof or exempt from pain. They think that taking their anger and frustration out on the person who loves them most is okay for some reason. In some odd way, they blame their wives for their own unhappiness and this is their way of striking back.

I am clear that I am against gay men marrying or staying married to straight women. Do I make this as a 100 percent statement or are there shades of gray here? Yes, there are shades of gray, but not enough of them to make me change my mind. If women are happy being married to their gay husbands, then more power to them. I have heard reasons why some of these women feel this way and I accept it. Each woman has her own set of issues and needs. But don't think for one moment that just because a handful of women have expressed this happiness that it changes my mind one iota. I am not here for the happy women—I am here for the suffering women. And the handful of happy women gives false hopes to the 98 percent of the unhappy women. That's why I don't pay much attention to them. There are people who survive nuclear wars, but I wouldn't want to be one of them if I had my choice. I don't want to walk on a minefield loaded with bombs to see if I can survive it. I'd rather skip that walk and take the safe road home.

I believe that the beauty of life is that each day offers us a new opportunity to wake up and change our lives for the better. No woman was born to suffer. Stuff happens that is beyond our control, but that doesn't mean at some point we can't take control.

And most importantly, I had an epiphany. It happened last year when I first started talking to my friend Jay who has written for me earlier in the book. Jay and I met in the spring of 2001 when he first found my website and wrote to me how he wished he had found it years before. Jay was divorced from his long-term wife and had moved on with his life with a wonderful man. We took an immediate liking to each other and a wonderful friendship has developed. Through his writing to me about his feelings during his marriage, he was able to help me verbalize what I felt was the one most important factor about these marriages. I wrote about it in my newsletter in the spring of 2001, and I still view these words as my most powerful:

Who would we be today if we had a straight husband? How would our destiny have changed if we were loved, nurtured, sexually desired with passion and tenderness, given emotional support and encouragement, and made to feel like we were part of a real couple in tune with each other's needs, wants, and aspirations? What if we didn't have to spend countless hours each day wondering why we were failures as wives, women, and lovers—ripping away our self-esteem layer by layer until we became strangers unto ourselves and others? What if our husbands' dishonesty and cheating didn't change us to become untrusting, suspicious, and doubting wives, forcing us to question our ability to make rational decisions? How many of us were sidetracked through those "detours of deceit" that diverted us from the direction that life might have taken otherwise?

Bottom line—no matter how much a gay man loves a straight woman, it is not the kind of love that fulfills the basic human need that all of us have. It can never be the kind of love that inspires the music that becomes classics or the poetry that makes the heart flutter. It is not the kind of love that can ever be returned to the degree that you are giving it. Even the best of relationships are barely more than great friendships—not the passion and excitement that make us thrive and look forward to waking up each day. And even these relationships are woven with dishonesty, distrust, infidelity, resentment, and frustration. Life was not meant to be this complicated.

Ah, of all of the words I have written, these were my favorites. It says it all. It's hard to dispute these words. I love them, and I hope they inspire you to make the right choices in your future!

Most importantly, the end is only a beginning. Remember-- repeat my new mantra:

**Life was never meant
to be this complicated.
Period.**

About the Author

Bonnie Kaye is an internationally recognized relationship counselor/author in the field of straight/gay marriages. She has provided relationship counseling and advice for nearly 30 years to more than 75,000 women who have sexually dysfunctional husbands due to homosexuality, bisexuality, or sexual addictions. She is considered an authority in this field by other professionals and the media. Kaye has published seven books on straight/gay relationships, which have sold thousands of copies. Her website **www.Gayhusbands.com** has consistently remained in the number one position on Google, Yahoo, and other major search engines since its launching in the year of 2000. When media contacts want an expert, they go to Bonnie Kaye who has more experience and expertise than any other person in the United States. Her official book website is located at **www.BonnieKayeBooks.com**. Kaye's support network has over 7,000 women around the world who receive her free monthly newsletter. She also has online computer support chat as well as a weekly internet radio show on Sundays, *Straight Wives Talk Show* on www.Blogtalkradio.com that can be accessed 24/7 around the world via the computer.

Kaye's other books include: *The Gay Husband Checklist for Women Who Wonder; Straight Wives: Shattered Lives (Volumes 1 and 2); ManReaders: A Woman's Guide to Dysfunctional Men; Bonnie Kaye's Straight Talk; How I Made My Husband Gay: Myths About Straight Wives;* and *Over the Cliff: Gay Husbands in Straight Marriages.*

CPSIA information can be obtained at www.ICGtesting.com
Printed in the USA
BVOW02s1436180915

418454BV00001B/10/P